FOLLOW ME
AS I FOLLOW
CHRIST

FOLLOW ME AS I FOLLOW CHRIST

A GUIDE FOR TEACHING CHILDREN IN A CHURCH SETTING

CHERYL DUNLOP

MOODY PUBLISHERS
CHICAGO

All Scripture quotations, unless otherwise indicated, are taken from the *New King James Version*. Copyright © 1982 by Thomas Nelson, Inc. Used by permission. All rights reserved.

Scripture quotations marked KJV are taken from the King James Version.

Scripture quotations marked NASB are taken from the *New American Standard Bible®*, © Copyright The Lockman Foundation 1960, 1962, 1963, 1968, 1971, 1972, 1973, 1975, 1977, 1994, and 1995. Used by permission.

Scripture quotations marked NIV are taken from the *Holy Bible, New International Version®*. NIV®. Copyright © 1973, 1978, 1984 by International Bible Society. Used by permission of Zondervan Publishing House. All rights reserved.

Library of Congress Cataloging-in-Publication Data

Dunlop, Cheryl J.
    Follow me as I follow Christ: a guide for teaching children in a church setting / by Cheryl J. Dunlop.
        p. cm.
    Includes bibliographical references.
    ISBN 0-8024-1094-4
    1. Christian education—Teaching methods. I. Title.

    BV1534 D834 2000
    268'.432—dc21

We hope you enjoy this book from Moody Publishers. Our goal is to provide high-quality, thought-provoking books and products that connect truth to your real needs and challenges. For more information on other books and products written and produced from a biblical perspective, go to www.moodypublishers.com or write to:

Moody Publishers
820 N. LaSalle Boulevard
Chicago, IL 60610

3 5 7 9 10 8 6 4 2

Printed in the United States of America

To Irene Malanowski,
who loved me and encouraged me
when I was a scared, lonely, friendless twelve-year-old,
and for whom I vowed to name my first daughter—
Since I have no daughters, this book is yours instead, with my love

and

To Rosalie de Rosset,
who taught me English composition (and friendship 101)
when I was a timid, lonely, almost friendless college freshman,
and who later accepted me into her circle of friends—
I will always love you and value your friendship

CONTENTS

PART 4. The Purpose of Teaching

PART 5. Understanding and Preparing the Lesson

PART 6. Teaching the Lesson

PART 7. Applying the Lesson: Beyond the Classroom

ACKNOWLEDGMENTS

It's odd to be on the other side of the acknowledgments page. Usually I'm reading it to see if an author whose book I've edited appreciated my work enough to mention me by name! And now I get to be the one naming some people and forgetting others.

To keep up the backward way of doing things for one more paragraph, I want to mention some authors I've edited and, in the process, from whom I've learned a few things that are reflected in this book. Michael Horton's books *Beyond Culture Wars* and *Where in the World Is the Church?* have been instrumental in helping me realize how often we in Christendom trivialize God and sideline the message of Scripture for our own methods. I hope that this book is more careful as a result. Ron Hutchcraft's *Battle for a Generation,* though it deals with teenagers rather than children, strengthened my burden for teaching and my awareness of teaching's being a battlefield, not a playground. And Gary Bredfeldt's revision of Larry Richards's *Creative Bible Teaching* helped focus some of my musings when I was trying to figure out how a teacher could effectively apply the truths of Scripture.

My brother Ed has always been one of my heroes. For many years he has worked with children fulltime and in the last few years has begun to write practical books for teachers and novels for boys and girls. Our discussions about books and children have been delightful and informative. He reviewed most of this book in manuscript form and made helpful suggestions. Hope Toole, my sister, has been my partner from afar as we have prayed for each other's students and discussed our joys and frustrations in the classroom.

Ella Lindvall, valued colleague and skilled editor of this book, has added much to the process, especially her wisdom.

And I can't forget to mention three of my own favorite teachers, Linda South (junior high English), Edna Zuraw (courses at Child Evangelism Fellowship's Leadership Training Institute), and Rosalie de Rosset (college English and literature courses): Thank you for your example and for letting me into your lives. I hope my own writing and teaching are better for having known you.

INTRODUCTION

If you are a beginning teacher (or someone who is just thinking about teaching children), welcome to one of God's most challenging and (at least occasionally) most rewarding fields.

I started teaching Sunday school when I was thirteen years old, because of my mother's encouragement. As much as I loved the children, as carefully as I prepared each week, my youth and inexperience worked against me for years. I was a timid disciplinarian, and I knew little about the fine points of teaching. Today some of my work is with inner-city boys and girls, so I'm glad for the years in which I learned how to teach by teaching easier children in smaller classes. And I'm also glad that along the way I have been able to pick up some formal and informal training. I know how few church teachers receive any training for the task—and how tiny is the fraction receiving *adequate* training. I know also how much most teachers long to improve their skills and their effectiveness.

A few months ago I attended a friend's church with her. Her church is bigger, and a bit more formal, than mine. The sixteen elders sat, eight on a side, on two front pews. When it came time for Communion, they filed out of their pews with even spacing between themselves—much like bridesmaids in a wedding. As they approached the Communion table and picked up the elements, each fell into step with a partner. They walked down the aisle, each pair in step, spaced perfectly from the two in front of them. Some of the men headed toward the balcony, some to the side aisles. Clearly, they had done this before. As I watched, I thought, *I wish churches trained their Sunday school teachers as well as they train these men!*

That is why this book was written. I want it to be a sort of teacher training series in book form. It is designed for you to read one "lesson" each week, then look to see how what you have learned can apply to your preparation, your teaching, or your interaction with individual children that week. If you do that consistently, I think you will find by the end of the year that you are more confident and that your perspective and your teaching have both changed a bit. Each reading ends with two questions or suggestions—sometimes for thought, sometimes for evaluation of some area of your teaching, sometimes for action. You may want to read the book with pencil in hand, underlining points that catch your attention, so that you can refer to it later as a handbook.

God has not given me my own children, but through the years He has loaned me hundreds of children, in settings ranging from camp counseling to teaching Sunday school, club programs, or vacation Bible school; from baby-sitting to interacting with neighborhood children who come by my house to read or make cookies. I have been awakened in the middle of the night to find my hair wet because the child in the bunk above me at camp just wet her bed. I have taught a five-year-old who had the vocabulary of a three-year-old . . . except for the swear words he spoke around the lump of tobacco in his cheek. I have fought to earn a young girl's respect, then later received drawings from her with "I love you" scrawled on them. I have felt the indescribable joy of listening to a child pray to have Jesus forgive her sins. In short, I have had my life affected, for better or for worse, in many ways because I have let children into it.

In this book, I'll introduce you to a few of those boys and girls, although I have changed all their names and occasionally disguised their circumstances. As you read, we'll be going into homes, camp settings, and classrooms to get to know children. At each stop we'll look at what Scripture has to say. The boys and girls you meet here may remind you of other children you know—children who frustrate you, try your patience, test every rule . . . then challenge you with profound questions about God.

My philosophy of teaching will be clear throughout this book, but I want to mention it up front. Much of what has been written about teaching children suggests that Sunday school or other children's programs have to look like carnivals if they are to be effective. I do believe in keeping boys and girls interested, but I also believe love and good teaching are more important than frills. After all, our calling is really to capture children's hearts for God and make disciples—not to entertain them and prepare them to be good consumers of American goods or good advocates of an American mind-set.

Therefore, much of this guide will focus on what Scripture says and how to translate that in such a way that children will listen and understand. We will also explore what childhood is like today. We will discuss telling a story, applying a lesson, some methods of effective discipline, interacting with individual needy boys and girls, and even interacting with parents. In all of it, the goal is to help you and your students take your teaching beyond one hour on Sunday morning (or whenever it is you teach).

My heart aches for today's children. I long to see the boys and girls under my care choose to follow God—and to do so eagerly. I yearn to see other teachers armed with the knowledge of Scripture, delight in God, and strong love for boys and girls that are basic elements to effective teaching. I'm praying that this book may help equip you for such effectiveness.

PART 1

UNDERSTANDING GOD AND SCRIPTURE

If we approach the Bible with a stained-glass voice and emotional tremors that make the book seem "religious," in the most frightening sense of that word, chances are our children will escape at the first opportunity. Our prayers, too, must reflect that we are speaking with Someone who is real, not that we are making a speech.

—GLADYS HUNT,
Honey for a Child's Heart: The Imaginative Use of Books in Family Life (Grand Rapids: Zondervan, 1989), 100.

IS THAT GOD UNDER THAT MICROSCOPE?

Oh, the depth of the riches both of the wisdom and knowledge of God! How unsearchable are His judgments and His ways past finding out! "For who has known the mind of the Lord? Or who has become His counselor? Or who has first given to Him and it shall be repaid to him?"

(ROMANS 11:33–35)

It's 2:30 in the morning. Outside, a powerful thunderstorm keeps the sky lit up almost continually, and I can hear the soft sounds of heavy rain. Normally, I'd be asleep, but I have gotten out of bed to watch the lightning and listen to the rain and thunder that have kept me awake.

I cannot help but be reminded of the elderly Christian woman who was asked whether she wasn't terrified during her city's recent earthquake. No, she answered, with the attitude of one who finds the question odd—it reminded her of what a strong God cared for her.

After a January 1999 Chicago blizzard gave us the second largest snowfall in city history, a fellow church member said with a smile, "I think it's kinda neat that God can shut down a city of this size just by sending a little snow."

Those who do not believe in God after their observation of nature are without excuse, Paul tells us in Romans 1. The sounds of a thunderstorm or the tremors of an earthquake or a city-whitening snowfall do not point a person to the Cross, but the Bible says such things should point the unbeliever toward belief in a Creator.

Yet, it's more than God's power that is displayed in tonight's storm; an inch or two of rain is also "water[ing] the earth, and mak[ing] it bring forth and bud" (Isaiah 55:10), making sure that life will go on. It's all under the control of a God whose rainbow promises that He will never again destroy the entire earth by water.

As the rain settles to a light patter and the thunder and lightning grow further apart, I'm convicted of how often I think of God as though He were not much bigger than I am. I sometimes talk or act as though I believe He ought to adjust Himself to suit my whims. The Bible tells us that everything—from the seasons to my breath—is held together by the word of His power (Hebrews 1:3). How incredible that this majestic God usually displays His power in acts of grace! But Scripture makes clear that He is waiting, that someday His power will rip through heaven and earth in a way that will show His holiness and His wrath.

This is no tame God.

Sometimes our theology tries to gentle God, to hide His power not just behind the self-chosen love of the Cross but behind our own unbiblical concepts as well. God is love—but that love is bound to His holiness, a holiness that cannot overlook sin. That holiness and that love are seen together in the horrible beauty of the Cross. God's love is not a willy-nilly acceptance of anyone's ideas and anyone's actions.

How often do our words downplay God? How often do our lives say that He can fit in here or there but that rearranging everything to follow Him is just too much? How often does our teaching put the earthshaking Lord of the universe under a microscope, trying to analyze Him and figure Him out so that we may present a tidy, predictable God for children to know and believe? Charles Ryrie has pointed out,

> The knowledge of God differs from all other knowledge in that man can have this knowledge only as far as God reveals it. If God did not initiate the revelation of Himself, there would be no way for man to know Him. Therefore, a human being must put himself under God who is the object of his knowledge. In other scholarly endeavors, the human being often places himself above the object of his investigation, but not so in the study of God.[1]

Normally as we study and learn, our brains analyze and figure out data, discarding this bit of information as irrelevant or unnecessary or even untrue, keeping that fact for further study. When we read the Bible, it is God we study, but this God is our Creator, and this God will be our Judge. This God has revealed in Scripture who He is and who we are, not for our accumulation of trivial facts to win Sunday school contests, not for our own amusement but so that we can align our thoughts and our lives with who He is. So that we can worship Him in truth. So that we can bow before His power and rejoice in His undeserved love.

This is who we teach. May this God never seem boring. And when our students are bored, may we recognize and somehow communicate that the problem is in the learner or the teacher, never in the One studied. May we line up our lives before Him as those to be judged, never as those to do the judging.

My God, how endless is thy love!
Thy gifts are ev'ry evening new;
And morning mercies from above
Gently distil like early dew.

I yield my powers to thy command,
To thee I consecrate my days;

Perpetual blessings from thine hand
Demand perpetual songs of praise.
—Isaac Watts

Note

1. Charles Ryrie, *Basic Theology: A Popular Systematic Guide to Understanding Biblical Truth* (Chicago: Moody, 1999), 29.

For Evaluation

1. Has your willingness to study and learn about God been limited by your own sense of seeking excitement, your self-centeredness, or even your laziness? Confess that to God as sin, and realign yourself with Him.

2. Examine your teaching. Do you tend to hide God behind your own "bells and whistles"? Or do you present Scripture as a dry study to be endured?

WHO IS THIS GOD WE TEACH? Part One: God's Holiness

And the Lord passed before him and proclaimed,
"The Lord, the Lord God . . . by no means
clearing the guilty, visiting the iniquity of the
fathers upon the children and the children's
children to the third and the fourth generation."

(EXODUS 34:6–7)

It might be hard for the average unchurched child to piece together a definition of God from a quarter of attending Sunday school. We often assume students know who God is, so we use His name and move on. Unfortunately, the other Bible characters may seem far more interesting to our students because God is in the background. Students rarely get a vision of the grandness of God. Obviously He's someone important, but the child can't really figure out why, especially since all the stories are about other people. Eventually the kid who recently started attending church does notice that two people—"God" and "Jesus"—seem to be the answer to most of the questions the teacher asks. But there God's significance ends.

Digging beneath the Sunday school answers, who is this God we teach? Let's review quickly some of the things the Bible says about Him. In this chapter we'll focus on His holiness and other aspects of His greatness; in the next, we'll look at "the rest of the story"—His choice to love human beings.

He is Creator. Everything that exists came from Him either directly (plants, animals, man, water) or indirectly (what animals and humans have been able to do with His creation, such as building houses) (Psalm 33:6; John 1:3; Colossians 1:16; Revelation 4:11).

He is eternal. Not only will He never die, but He never had a beginning (Psalm 102:25–26; Malachi 3:6; 1 Corinthians 2:7; 1 Timothy 1:17).

He is independent. He does not need anything He has made (1 Kings 8:27; John 5:26). *He is all-powerful.* Nothing is too hard for Him (Psalms 33:9; 115:3; 135:6; Isaiah 46:10–11; Luke 1:37; Ephesians 1:19–20).

He is all-knowing. He is wise, and He knows everything that happens even before it happens (Psalm 147:5; Proverbs 15:3; Isaiah 46:10; John 2:25; Hebrews 4:13).

He is holy. He is absolutely pure and separate from sin and from sinners (Psalm 99:1–3, 9; Isaiah 40:18; 55:9; Habakkuk 1:13; Hebrews 10:31).

He is just. No sinner will get away with sin, but no one will be punished unjustly. Sin deserves death (Deuteronomy 32:4; Job 34:10; Jeremiah 9:24; Ezekiel 18:20; Romans 3:23; 6:23).

He is sovereign. Sovereign is a "king" word, and indeed God is King over everything—even Satan (Job 26:6–14; Psalms 115:3; 135:6; Isaiah 66:1; Lamentations 3:37–38; 1 Timothy 6:15).

It's interesting how much the Old Testament emphasizes God's holiness even as it looks ahead to the Redeemer—as though that emphasis is necessary in order for people to understand how much His love really means when it is finally shown fully on the Cross.

In Isaiah 6:5, we are told about the prophet Isaiah seeing God. Rather than bursting into a praise chorus, as we might expect him to do, he said, "Woe is me, for I am undone! Because I am a man of unclean lips, and I dwell in the midst of a people of unclean lips; for my eyes have seen the King, the Lord of hosts."

In Exodus, Moses suffered a devastating demotion. When he fled for his life after killing an Egyptian, he went from being an adopted member of Pharaoh's family to a shepherd in exile. It was probably a boring job, with plenty of time to look around at the same old desert he saw every day—until the day he saw a bush that was burning without being burned up. As he approached to look at it, God spoke.

His first words were not, "Moses, I love you." Moses needed to know who God was, and God chose to emphasize His holiness. He called Moses by name, then He warned him, "Do not draw near this place. Take your sandals off your feet, for the place where you stand is holy ground" (Exodus 3:5). When He said that, Moses hid his face, because he was rightly afraid to look at God—he would have died. Only then did God tell Moses the good news that He had come to deliver His people from slavery.

The story of Moses reminds us of the need to approach God reverently. That's not just an Old Testament principle. Hebrews 12:28 tells us of the need to "serve God acceptably with reverence and godly fear."

But those who know Christ are also reminded of the privilege we have to come as no one before His incarnation could even think of coming: boldly (Hebrews 4:16). We need Christ as a mediator, but we need no other mediator. We come boldly because God truly loves us and because through Christ we are truly forgiven—even to the point of being children of God Himself! (1 John 3:1).

How important is it that we teach a complete picture of who God is and not just the "nice" parts such as His love? God's holiness makes the Cross necessary. God's justice makes the Cross make sense. God's righteousness reminds us we cannot do anything for ourselves and that we're not doing God a favor by grudgingly coming to Him if He asks politely.

> If evangelists and preachers spent more time teaching about the true nature and character of God and less time trying to convince sinners of the advantage of coming to God, we would hear the question asked more often by repentant, anxious sinners, ". . . *Sirs, what must I do to be saved?*"[1] [Ellipses in original]

Note

1. Trevor McIlwain with Nancy Everson, *Firm Foundations: Building According to Plan,* children's edition, book 1 (Sanford, Florida: New Tribes Mission, 1993), 25–26.

For Further Study

1. Look up and read the Scripture verses listed next to the traits that describe who God is.

2. Why is God's holiness a good thing?

WHO IS THIS GOD WE TEACH?
Part Two:
God's Love

*And the Lord passed before him and proclaimed, "The
Lord, the Lord God, merciful and gracious,
longsuffering, and abounding in goodness and truth,
keeping mercy for thousands, forgiving iniquity and
transgression and sin."*

(EXODUS 34:6–7)

God is holy. That means He will always do the right thing. Unfortunately for human beings, the "right thing" includes eternal punishment for sin. The Bible emphasizes that "there is none who does good, no not one" (Romans 3:12). Since Ezekiel 18:4 tells us, "The soul that sinneth, it shall die" (KJV), we're in trouble. That's where the good news comes in. The Bible also tells us God is love, and He has made a way to take the punishment we deserve upon Himself. Let's look at a few more facts about Him.

God is merciful. He does not want to punish sinners, and He shows mercy (1 Chronicles 16:34; Psalms 57:10; 86:5; 136:1; Luke 13:34; Romans 6:23; Titus 3:4–7).

He is gracious. His grace found a way to punish His Son instead of the sinners who deserve His wrath (Ephesians 1:7; 2:8–9; Hebrews 1:3).

He is love. From the beauty around us, to the choice He made to communicate to human beings in Scripture, to His ultimate sacrifice of Jesus Christ on the Cross, His love shows up everywhere (Psalm 145:15–16; Isaiah 46:3–4; Matthew 5:45; John 3:16; Acts 14:17; Romans 5:8; James 1:17; 2 Peter 1:3).

He is faithful. He will do what He has promised (Psalm 89:1–2, 33–34; 1 Thessalonians 5:24; 2 Timothy 2:13; Hebrews 10:23).

He is true. He cannot lie (Numbers 23:19; Jeremiah 10:10; Romans 3:4; Hebrews 6:18).

How do we relate these truths to our lives? Because of God's holiness, He cannot be around our sin. Because of His love, He wants relationship with us. It's hard to teach both holiness and love at the same time, so most people lean toward one or the other. But the Gospel includes both sides, and we must also do so.

One year, the girls in my cabin at camp were quietly working on a devotional worksheet near bedtime. I was walking around, telling each girl to finish quickly, because I'd be turning the lights off soon. One girl, Alicia, was lying on her stomach with her head in her arms, and I assumed she was already asleep. As I was about to pass by her quietly, she raised her head and looked at me. Her eyes were wet with tears. I knelt beside her and asked, "What's wrong, honey?"

"Is it true," she asked, trying not to cry again, "that if you don't believe in Jesus, you'll die?" A boy at the camp had gotten that far in witnessing to her. She said she didn't know anything about the Bible, so she didn't know whether it was true.

"Yes, it's true," I said. Immediately she turned her face away. "But let me tell you the good news." I turned to Genesis and reviewed the stories of Creation and the Fall that had been taught earlier in the day. I explained the difference between physical and spiritual death. I explained that God said all have sinned—like Adam—and all deserve death. Then I turned to the Gospels and lingered over the solution to the problem, which is found only in Jesus.

I told her there was nothing she could do about her sin, but Jesus had already been punished for it. Her wet face glowed with a heartfelt smile as she heard the answer to her dilemma. But her prayer was hesitant: "*I hope* You will forgive my sins." Later in the week I was delighted to hear her bolder assurance as she told God: "Thank You for forgiving all the sins I have ever done."

For Further Study

1. Look up and read the Scripture verses listed next to the traits that describe who God is.

2. Why does God's holiness help us understand His love? Write in your own words what the true Gospel is.

TEACHING WHAT THE BIBLE TEACHES

*They received the word with all readiness, and
searched the Scriptures daily to find out whether
these things were so.*

(ACTS 17:11)

I was flipping through a children's Bible story book at a bookstore when I came across Solomon's story. I read it casually, but my attention was caught by the author's application for the child: "Pray and ask God to make you as wise as Solomon." A child is unlikely to think of such a presumptuous prayer on his own, but an author casually threw it into a book for boys and girls without thinking of the ramifications of suggesting an unbiblical prayer a child might pray the way he'd ask a wish from a genie.

What does Scripture say? God told Solomon, "See, I have given you a wise and understanding heart, so that there has not been anyone like you before you, *nor shall any like you arise after you*" (1 Kings 3:12, italics added). The Bible is quite clear that Solomon was given special wisdom as a favor from God. Though God has promised us necessary wisdom (James 1:5), He has not made us the same offer He made to Solomon. God does not offer miracles free for the asking.

It's a little thing, really. It was a cheap book published by a secular publisher and being sold on a discount table in an out-of-the-way bookstore. But it reminded me of the dangers that can arise when we use words carelessly, especially with boys and girls. A child is dependent upon adults to lay the foundation for his understanding of the Bible, and foundations are too important to be laid carelessly. A child can be led astray by such teaching.

I was in a church service where the congregation nonchalantly sang to God, "Let Your glory fall in this room." Probably not one in fifty people recognized how extraordinary a request they were making in a song casually sung.

A teacher was drawing a diagram on the chalkboard as he explained that no good works can get us to heaven. He drew the line representing "reading the Bible" a little longer than he drew the others, as he said jokingly, "Reading the Bible almost gets us there." A little downward swoop of the chalk showed that that deed wasn't quite good enough, either. I knew he wasn't serious, but I wondered if the children would know that, and I winced at what he had carelessly introduced into an otherwise clear presentation of the Gospel. Several days later I heard a child explaining what she had learned earlier that week. "I learned that reading the Bible can almost get us to heaven," she said seriously. Careless use of humor had given the false idea that reading the Bible gives us merit with God that helps us earn salvation.

Have I ever confused boys and girls by similar careless statements—or even confused them when they heard me wrong because of my sloppy pronunciation or unclear wording? Have I presented erroneous information as a result of misreading Scripture or forgetting what the Bible teaches on some subject? Have I answered a question the child didn't ask, leading to confusion and misunderstanding regarding the question he did ask? It's easy for a teacher to do any of these things. I pray that God will keep me from such errors. He uses imperfect teachers every time He uses human teachers. Nevertheless, the warnings given in Scripture to teachers prove that such mistakes are not minor ones (see Mark 9:42; James 3:1).

The apostle Paul was chosen by God to write almost half the New Testament, yet his congregation in Berea is praised for checking everything he said against Scripture to be sure it was true (Acts 17:11).

Often when the teacher teaches something other than what the Bible teaches, it's because the curriculum she uses does so. If you look at any curriculum carefully, you are apt to find quite a few examples of such. Most of the time they are minor, but the discerning teacher should still make every attempt to teach what the Bible teaches rather than relying on what the teacher's guide teaches. For example, the story of Jonah has the clear point of God's mercy toward sinners and wayward saints, and it deals with the irresistibility of God's call in a believer's life. But I have heard the lesson taught to emphasize God's forcing Jonah to deal with racism. When redemption is the "moral" of a biblical story, is it OK to make it say something else instead? And as much as Jonah may have disliked the extremely cruel enemies of his people, do we have any evidence that actual racism was involved? The story can be applied to point out that our witnessing should not be limited to people we like or those who are like us, but the passage is not about racism.

The risk is greater anytime a teacher goes into class with an "agenda." Perhaps he knows that many students in his class are struggling with a particular sin or have a particular need, and he thinks he sees a place where the Scripture for the day can be used to speak to that issue. But Scripture doesn't have detailed solutions to every problem we face. Scripture's primary role is to lead us to salvation and knowledge of God. Moral guidance is secondary. As we'll explore more when we get into preparing and teaching a lesson, paying attention to what the passage does say will protect us from teaching our children something it doesn't.

For Thought

1. When have you forced an application to meet a perceived need in your class?

2. In what areas of the Bible do you need clearer understanding yourself (for example, Jesus' life, or the Jewish background to the Old Testament, or a particular book of the Bible)? Ask your pastor or a trusted Christian friend how you can get help exploring that area.

CHILDREN AND MAJESTY

And without controversy great is the mystery of
godliness: God was manifested in the flesh,
justified in the Spirit, seen by angels, preached
among the Gentiles, believed on in the world,
received up in glory.

(1 TIMOTHY 3:16)

"Did Jesus really do that? Cool!" Brandon, eyes wide and mouth open, stared at me. If Jesus could make Lazarus come back to life, then He is better than . . . well, than Superman and the Easter Bunny and Santa Claus put together!

Children are born worshipers; they intuitively sense that God is even greater than Mommy and Daddy. Young children aren't looking for God to be their buddy. They sense their distance from Him. They know how weak they are, and they are reassured to know that He is big enough to take care of them. They come with awe to Him when they learn He loves them enough to *want* to care for them. "Now to the King eternal, immortal, invisible, to God who alone is wise, be honor and glory for ever and ever. Amen" (1 Timothy 1:17).

Have you ever noticed that God *enjoys* children's praises? One day religious leaders asked Jesus to put His littlest followers in their place: "But when the chief priests and scribes saw the wonderful things that He did, and the children crying out in the temple and saying, 'Hosanna to the Son of David!' they were indignant and said to Him, 'Do You hear what these are saying?'" I can imagine a smile on His face when He pointed them back to Scripture, saying, "Yes. Have you never read, 'Out of the mouth of babes and nursing infants You have perfected praise'?" (Matthew 21:15–16). "Yes," Jesus was saying, "I do indeed hear these children praising Me. And it's the best sound I can imagine."

We live in a culture with short-lived heroes. Each Christmas brings a new must-have toy. The most loved TV series fades in popularity. And children soon develop skepticism toward authority and cynicism about the idea of anyone's being greater than they are. If boys and girls are to grow to adulthood with a sense of God's majesty, their parents and teachers need to encourage that sense while the children are still young enough to worship spontaneously.

Ironically, for many of the church's teachers that means resisting the urge to bring God down to a level where youngsters can "understand" Him. We worship God before we can begin to comprehend Him, and we will have all of eternity to learn more about Him. Ditties and chants may make a club program feel more like a party, but be careful lest in the celebration the majesty of God gets lost.

Come with me to a classroom where two dozen first through third graders were participating in children's church on Easter Sunday. For twenty minutes, according to curriculum instructions, each child led his or her partner blindfolded among three small plastic clowns tossed onto the floor. (The point of the exercise was unclear.) The next twenty minutes were spent making finger puppets. The last twenty minutes was the lesson, the Resurrection. The finger puppets "walked" with the women as they went to the tomb and "celebrated" with them by moving up and down when the women found the tomb empty.

The curriculum then had the teacher hand around a rock and tell the students to rub it on their palms. She asked what it felt like (rough). She said if they rubbed it on their hands really hard, they could scratch themselves quite badly. She told the children that Jesus was hurt very badly. But can the agony of the Crucifixion be made so user-friendly? Christ died a vicious death—absolutely beyond comparison to a scratch.

The teacher asked the class what a rock did when it was put in water. She put this one in water, and it sank. Then—because the rock was volcanic—it came back up. She pointed out that that was what Jesus did—He came back up, contrary to expectations. She ended by stating what was apparently the curriculum's application of the lesson: "When we know Jesus, nothing can keep us down."

But is the Resurrection really just a clever story to teach us resilience? Or is it God's victory over Satan and over our sin, the affirmation that what Christ did on the cross can indeed cancel all my wickedness, the triumph of God on which the church was built? And if we must somehow try to "experience" what it was like to be part of an encounter that is far too big for our imaginations, should we do so by scratching our palms and waving finger puppets?

I hasten to emphasize that the problem here was *not with the teacher but basically with curriculum* that was trying too hard to be "creative" and "relevant" and in the process forgetting appropriate reverence and awe. But teachers need to know how to critique curriculum and reject all such unbiblical teaching.

The entire church is built upon the truth of the Resurrection. A lifetime of celebrating Easter can't exhaust its excitement. Yet trivial "celebrations" of it in childhood may inoculate one against its power. And unbelieving boys and girls can walk out of such a classroom without any idea of why Jesus allowed Himself to be killed.

Young children may have few alternatives to church, but in a few years their choices will overwhelm them. Meanwhile, it is part of the teacher's job to introduce them to a God who is big enough for their worship and awe. A God who is bigger than gang solidarity and sweet-talking boyfriends and pounding music. A God who is worthy of their respect and awe, not a god to be outgrown.

God *is* big enough for your children's worship and awe. Scripture gives unending affirmations of that. The God of the Bible isn't always user-friendly or fun, but He is certainly never boring. He's much more three-dimensional than the cardboard Christ some find easier to teach. He's much more likely to convict of sin than a more fun Jesus would be. But the God of the Bible is worthy of worship. A simplified Jesus is not even worth Sunday morning's lost sleep.

If God seems boring, either because Sunday school is boring or because Sunday school is so delightful and distracting that Scripture itself seems dull, then children will outgrow church. Children outgrow making things out of construction paper. They outgrow singing "Father Abraham." But if a child is stunned by the power and love of God, will he outgrow Him?

For Thought

1. What recent examples from your class show you that children love to worship God?

2. What are three specific ways you can encourage your students in worship and understanding of the greatness of God?

WHAT SCRIPTURE SAYS ABOUT CHILDREN

*All your children shall be taught by the Lord, and great
shall be the peace of your children.*

(ISAIAH 54:13)

Children are an afterthought in many church programs. When evangelism is discussed or taught, many people think only of the adult potential convert. Yet most Christians came to faith as children. Most of us learned of Christ the same way Timothy did—at the knee of a mother, grandmother, or other adult who taught us in childhood.

Scripture has much more to say about children than many adults realize. Let's look at a few of those verses.

Children are capable of believing faith.

"And whoever causes one of *these little ones who believe in Me* to stumble, it would be better for him if a millstone were hung around his neck, and he were thrown into the sea." (Mark 9:42, italics added)

"From childhood you have known the Holy Scriptures, which are able to make you wise for salvation through faith which is in Christ Jesus." (2 Timothy 3:15)

"Remember now your Creator in the days of your youth." (Ecclesiastes 12:1)

"But when the chief priests and scribes saw the wonderful things that He did, and the children crying out in the temple and saying, 'Hosanna to the Son of David!' [which suggests that the children recognized Christ as the Messiah] they were indignant." (Matthew 21:15)

Children should be included in gatherings of the community of faith.

"Gather the people together, men and women and little ones, . . . that they may hear and that they may learn to fear the Lord your God and carefully observe all the words of this law." (Deuteronomy 31:12)

"Now all Judah, with their little ones, their wives, and their children, stood before the Lord." (2 Chronicles 20:13)

"Now while Ezra was praying, and while he was confessing, weeping, and bowing down before the house of God, a very large congregation of men, women, and children assembled to him from Israel; for the people wept very bitterly." (Ezra 10:1)

"Gather the people, sanctify the congregation, assemble the elders, gather the children and nursing babes." (Joel 2:16)

Children should be deliberately taught.

"You shall teach them diligently to your children, and shall talk of them when you sit in your house, when you walk by the way, when you lie down, and when you rise up." (Deuteronomy 6:7)

"We will not hide them from their children, telling to the generation to come the praises of the Lord, and His strength and His wonderful works that He has done." (Psalm 78:4)

(See also Exodus 12:26–27; Deuteronomy 11:18–21; Psalms 71:17; 78:5–6; Proverbs 22:6; Ephesians 6:1–4; Colossians 3:20.)

Children can be used by God.

Three stories quickly come to mind: Naaman's slave girl (2 Kings 5:1–15); the boy with the loaves and fishes whose lunch Jesus multiplied (John 6:5–14); and John the Baptist, filled with the Holy Spirit even in his mother's womb (Luke 1:41–44).

Children are held accountable by God.

"Even a child is known by his deeds, by whether what he does is pure and right." (Proverbs 20:11)

"And the child Samuel grew in stature, and in favor both with the Lord and men." (1 Samuel 2:26)

(For rather scary examples, see Deuteronomy 21:18; 2 Kings 2:23–24; also see 1 Samuel 2:18; 3:4–15.)

Children can serve as examples to adults.

"Therefore whoever humbles himself as this little child is the greatest in the kingdom of heaven." (Matthew 18:4)

God holds adults accountable for their actions toward children.

"And whoever causes one of these little ones who believe in Me to stumble, it would be better for him if a millstone were hung around his neck, and he were thrown into the sea." (Mark 9:42)

"Take heed that you do not despise one of these little ones, for I say to you that in heaven their angels always see the face of My Father who is in heaven." (Matthew 18:10)

God loves children.

"Leave your fatherless children, I will preserve them alive; and let your widows trust in Me." (Jeremiah 49:11)

"Let the little children come to Me, and do not forbid them; for of such is the kingdom of heaven." (Matthew 19:14)

"Whoever receives one of these little children in My name receives Me; and whoever receives Me, receives not Me but Him who sent Me." (Mark 9:37)

Children are gifts from God, especially to their families.
"Behold, children are a heritage from the Lord, the fruit of the womb is His reward." (Psalm 127:3)

The Bible also records numerous miracles involving children. Here are a few.
Elijah raises a widow's son from the dead. (1 Kings 17:17–23)
Elijah's successor, Elisha, also raises a widow's son from the dead. (2 Kings 4:1–37)
Jesus heals a demon-possessed boy. (Matthew 17:14–18)
Jesus raises a twelve-year-old girl from the dead. (Mark 5:38–42)

Human parenting is an example of divine parenting.
"If you then, being evil, know how to give good gifts to your children, how much more will your heavenly Father give the Holy Spirit to those who ask Him!" (Luke 11:13)
"No discipline seems pleasant at the time, but painful. Later on, however, it produces a harvest of righteousness and peace for those who have been trained by it." (Hebrews 12:11 NIV)
Biblically, teaching children is far more than just baby-sitting. James warns us that teaching itself is a calling that we dare not take lightly: "My brethren, let not many of you become teachers, knowing that we shall receive a stricter judgment" (3:1). It's a serious calling—and a priceless one.

For Further Study

1. Take time to read Matthew 18–19. What does Jesus say about children?

2. Look up a few of the references above that are listed but not quoted. Which of the passages in this chapter give a different perspective than you thought Scripture gave?

UNDERSTANDING CHILDREN AND THEIR WORLD

We can't expect our children to resist the gods of this world unless we equip them—and ourselves—with knowledge of, and trust in, a true God who is strong enough to be worth turning to, away from what fascinates their peers.

—MARVA J. DAWN,
Is It a Lost Cause? Having the Heart of God for the Church's Children (Grand Rapids: Eerdmans, 1997), 22.

THE SOUL OF A CHILD

I have no greater joy than to hear that
my children walk in truth.

(3 JOHN 4)

Years ago I had a young friend named Becky. Becky craved adult attention, and she literally clung to me for minutes at a time when she had the chance. Like many children, she seemed to have a hard time offering genuine apologies. When I asked her to apologize to a child she had somehow hurt or offended, she offered a quick "sorry" without even looking at the other child.

One day Becky made cookies at my house. During the course of the baking, she made three or four childish errors, including getting a bit of cookie dough on the table. Each time, she said, "I'm sorry, Cheryl," in a manner that suggested she expected punishment. Finally I sorrowfully put my arm around her and said, "Becky, it's never fair for me to get mad at you for an accident."

The next day, Becky was in my house briefly. As I tried to send her out the door, she stalled by taking some pieces of candy from the table. I told her to put them back, but she acted as though she thought I was playing. Finally I squatted to her level and said firmly, "Give me the candy. It's time for you to go."

Instead of obeying, she threw herself on me in a hug. I caught her but was knocked off balance. Before I could regain my equilibrium, she threw herself at me again. This time, I sprawled backward in unladylike fashion as I tried desperately not to let Becky fall and hurt herself and not to hit my head on the glass of the buffet directly behind me.

I sat up, and quietly Becky handed me the candy. I said, "OK, I'll see you another time." Then her eyes looked at me sadly, and her head hung down. I asked softly, "What's wrong?"

She looked up and said quietly, "I'm sorry I made you fall." I wasn't sure whether her sadness came from fear, guilt, or a combination. She may have been afraid I'd get angry, and she clearly feared rejection. I thought back to my words from the day before. Both of us knew my falling had been caused by her deliberate action, not by an accident. And she waited to hear whether I could forgive an act of minor mischief and carelessness.

I put my hands on her head and said, "It's OK." Then I brought her head against mine and said, "I forgive you." Becky danced out of the house with the spirit of a child who knows she is forgiven.

We adults tend to rationalize our sins away, but since rationalization doesn't really work, our sense of being forgiven often doesn't feel very deep either. But as Becky danced out through my front door, I trembled with the awe of holding some responsibility for a child's moral and spiritual training. I sensed what it's like to hold a child's soul in one's hand and know that one little moment can be life-changing.

In this section, we will be taking a closer look at the world of a child. Some of what we explore may be distressing to read. Satan is not compassionate or just; he is very involved with today's children. Whether it's introducing them to drugs or gun violence, his tools are well honed. But on the positive side, children have a greater capacity for trust than adults do, and they can know God deeply. We will spend time later in this section rejoicing over the opportunities God has given us to work with people in this critical part of life—childhood.

For Thought

1. Make a list of the groups of children you influence (for example, your class, relatives, neighbor children, your children's friends).

2. On a single sheet of paper, write the names of particular children you influence and place that sheet where you will see it often—perhaps on your refrigerator or in the front of your Bible. Over the weeks ahead, as you go through this book, look at your list and pray for the boys and girls God has put in your life.

CHILDREN WITHOUT CHILDHOOD

*I do not pray that You should take them out
of the world, but that You should keep them
from the evil one. . . . Sanctify them by Your
truth. Your word is truth.*

(JOHN 17:15, 17)

Many authors have recently noted the gradual erosion of childhood innocence in society.[1] Multiple factors add to this trend: television and the movie industry's bringing violence and sexual knowledge to young children; the Internet's pornography; video games that allow boys and girls hands-on experience in violence; the fact that ever younger children are listening to the hardest music; latchkey children who are left unsupervised for many hours; explicit, permissive sex education in school; warnings from parents and teachers about what "stranger dangers" might do to careless kids, leading them to distrust adults; the erosion of the idea that children deserve to be protected from violent or sexual words and images; and the breakdown of the community system whereby neighbors hold each other's kids accountable.

More possibilities could be named. But take away adult guidance, and leave children to be raised by other kids and the media—both of which often assault their innocence by glorifying rebellion and making depravity "cool"—and you have the makings of a culture that exists without childhood.

Consider the ramifications of the following news items:

- the murder of child beauty queen JonBenet Ramsey
- the teacher who bore two children fathered by her teenage student
- the death of seven-year-old "pilot" Jessica Dubroff
- the eleven- and thirteen-year-olds convicted of killing a teacher and five students in their schoolyard after pulling the fire alarm
- the two teenagers who planted thirty bombs in their Colorado high school and shot twelve students and a teacher before committing suicide
- the seven- and eight-year-old Chicago boys who were held falsely for the murder of an eleven-year-old girl

Many other items could make the list, but these demonstrate how much our images of childhood have changed and how much childhood itself has changed.

I have seen enough in my own encounters with boys and girls to agree that childhood is disappearing fast:

- A girl about six told me casually that her aunt told her never to get in a car with a pimp because pimps "want you to have a lot of men."
- Two girls going into fifth grade, not yet in puberty, were walking to the park with a group of church kids when a musclebound man in his twenties walked by. Both girls' heads swiveled. They looked him over, then one girl commented to the other, "He has a nice butt."
- Junior-age boys at a Christian camp, bored by waiting during an outside game, started pulling down each other's pants.
- A child going into third grade told me nonchalantly that she didn't know whether she'd wait for marriage to have sex.
- Childhood swearing has become commonplace.
- A sixth-grade girl asked a fourth grader if she was "going out" with a certain boy, then insisted the fourth grader at least "liked" him.
- I have had to "chaperone" a six-year-old boy and his eleven-year-old girlfriend as they looked for opportunities to be alone.
- A slim ten-year-old girl who had not yet begun to develop physically bemoaned how "fat" she was.
- A fourth grader ticked off his schedule of almost nightly events and told me he had too much stress.
- Traffic was moving slowly on a busy Chicago street because two boys about ten were amusing themselves riding their bikes in slow wide circles in the street while three younger girls sat on the curb and watched.

Childhood has often been falsely romanticized. Children *aren't* always sweet; they taunt in cruel ways children they don't like. They aren't always honest; they learn how to get away with lying at an early age. They avoid work if they can. They fight with their siblings. They take more pieces of candy than the teacher said they may have—if they think she won't notice. Johann Christoph Blumhardt said, "There is a fight against the evil of the world, and nowhere is this fight seen more clearly than in children."[2]

In the past, the adult world always conspired to help children learn trust and to protect them from secrets too big for them.[3] Not anymore. Boys and girls see many adults divorcing, and they fear their parents will be next. They hear on the news about rapes and brutal murders, child abuse and starvation. They see children a few years older than themselves selling drugs. They see on the news that kids a few years older than they are have been arrested for murder. They hear about schoolyard shootings and molested children. They see titillating pictures on the Internet. Adults yell at them, using the "F" word. Children long for security, but the adult world pursues rapid change, so most boys and girls move every few years, and many shuttle back and forth between estranged parents.

Worst of all, perhaps, is that adults have abdicated their authority. Children used to find security in knowing that grown-ups had authority and, with it, responsibility for their well-being. Now adults hesitate to admit they know more than children do, apparently for fear of "hurting their self-esteem." Schools encourage students to set their own learning goals and make their own classroom rules. Sex-education classes encourage adolescents to discover their own sexual standards. Boys and girls belligerently act as if they do indeed know more than adults do. And they are saddled with responsibility they are far too young to handle.

What are some protective steps a caring teacher can take in relating to his or her students?

- Give them the security of knowing you are in charge and, therefore, they don't need to be.
- Be mature and consistent, loving and firm.
- Protect them from each other and teach them love. Be aware of negative peer influence and counteract it.
- Don't allow inappropriate conversation or language.
- Know what your students face at home (mothers' live-in boyfriends, pornography, unsupervised television viewing, etc.).
- Pray for your students.
- Show them enthusiastic love, and be part of their lives.

Notes

1. See, for example, Neil Postman, *The Disappearance of Childhood* (New York: Vintage, 1982, 1994); Diane and Michael Medved, *Saving Childhood: Protecting Our Children from the National Assault on Innocence* (New York: HarperCollins, 1998); William Kilpatrick, *Why Johnny Can't Tell Right from Wrong and What We Can Do About It* (New York: Touchstone, 1992).
2. Johann Christoph Blumhardt and Christoph Friedrich Blumhardt, *Thoughts About Children* (Rifton, N.Y.: Plough, 1980), 55.
3. This point is developed well in Postman, *Disappearance of Childhood*.

For Evaluation

1. In what ways have you been placing adult expectations on the children in your class?

2. How can you protect your boys and girls from childhood-eroding influences?

NOT A SENTIMENTAL AFFAIR

*Then He said to His disciples, "The harvest
truly is plentiful, but the laborers are few.
Therefore pray the Lord of the harvest to send
out laborers into His harvest."*

(MATTHEW 9:37)

At six, Victoria was responsible for little sister Patty. Both girls had strong sweet odors and dirty faces. Victoria never smiled and never relaxed, but four-year-old Patty was an affectionate, beautiful child with a turned-up nose and an eager, intelligent face. Victoria was rough and surly. Her brown hair was not cut straight, and every few minutes she pushed it out of her eyes. She mistreated her younger sister. She was rude to other children her age. She tried to boss me around. Her scowl deepened if I touched her.

I rarely saw the girls' mother. Whenever she had a boyfriend in, she locked the girls out, so I usually saw them during such visits. Once in a while she came down the street to tell them they could come back, but usually they wandered the street with their wagon of new toys until they got bored and decided to see if they were allowed back home. I never turned them away when they came to my door, so they soon came every day or two. They tried to climb the trellis, jumped on the bed, and broke every other household rule. When they left, I was usually tired.

Victoria preferred violent games—games with witches and monsters—and I did my best to redirect her interests. She yelled when things didn't go her way. She pulled away or hit at the slightest physical contact. I was a teenager when I knew her, and I was naive. As an adult, I remember that child with new eyes, for I realize that some of her mother's boyfriends probably handled her in ways little girls should not be touched. Her belligerent, antisocial behavior, her aversion to touch, and the household in which she lived suggest strongly the possibility of sexual abuse.[1]

One day the girls proudly brought their new dog, a purebred blond cocker spaniel. They liked my cocker, and their mother had bought them one of their own. Sometimes they hugged their dog; sometimes they dragged it at the end of its leash. But they still came to see me and my crayfish (my "crab") or play with my cocker.

After having to send Victoria home a few times (reluctantly), I eventually earned her respect. One time I walked out into the front yard with the sisters, and Victoria quietly slipped her arm around me. It was the only sign of affection I remember receiving from her, but that made it all the more significant.

When adults remember childhood, often it's with thoughts of holidays, birthdays, toys, and bedtime stories. Yet much of childhood is deeply traumatic even in the most ideal families: lost friends, bad report cards, injuries, moves, sibling rivalry, punishment. Even the best childhood is a time of insecurity: Do my parents really love me? What will happen if I wet my pants during class like Tommy did? Will that big dog bite me? Does my best friend like me anymore? Will I pass the math test? Will I get a spanking if Mom and Dad find out what I did?

For many boys and girls, childhood itself is something to be outgrown as quickly as possible. Latchkey children, kids in daycare for long hours, kids in violently combative homes, children of extreme poverty, friendless children, children who are beaten or sexually molested, or those who are left unprotected in dangerous homes or given adult-sized responsibilities such as caring for numerous younger siblings—all these situations can make children long to leave childhood limitations behind.

I often think about Victoria and Patty. I've prayed through the years that God would bring along others to love them and to tell them of Christ, that He would protect their purity, that He would work in their mother's heart, and that He would erase some of the effects of the evils done against them. They are adults now, and I pray for them as adults. Yet I still picture them as children. I often wonder how many neighbors saw only the wagonful of toys and thought nostalgically of childhood when Victoria and Patty went by.

Children can be cute. They can be sweet, and affectionate, and innocent. But often the teacher's task is doing battle against Satan for the boys and girls he tries to claim as his own. Enjoy them, and love them—but learn to listen for their hurts rather than seeing their lives through the grid of what childhood is "supposed to be like."

Note

1. A letter to Ann Landers does a good job of summarizing "the signs of childhood sexual abuse—belligerent, antisocial or sexually explicit behavior, nightmares, isolation, depression, self-mutilation and attempts at suicide." Signed D.C., Prospect, Ky., Ann Landers, "Be aware of signs of child sexual abuse" (*Chicago Tribune*, 21 December 1998; sec. 5, p. 3).

For Further Study

1. To find out more about the difficult side of childhood today, read at least one of the following books: William Kilpatrick, *Why Johnny Can't Tell Right from Wrong and What We Can Do About It* (New York: Touchstone, 1992); Neil Postman, *The Disappearance of Childhood* (New York: Vintage, 1982, 1994); Glenda Revell, *Glenda's Story: Led by Grace* (Lincoln, Neb.: Gateway to Joy, 1994); Michael and Diane Medved, *Saving Childhood: Protecting Our Children from the National Assault on Innocence* (New York: HarperCollins, 1998).

2. If you know a person who teaches in a public school or otherwise interacts with other people's children full-time, ask him or her, "In what ways is childhood different today than when you were growing up?"

10

DEVELOPING
A BROKEN
HEART

*Can a woman forget her nursing child, and
not have compassion on the son of her
womb? Surely they may forget, yet I will
not forget you.*

(ISAIAH 49:15)

*For death has come through our windows,
has entered our palaces, to kill off the
children—no longer to be outside! And the
young men—no longer on the streets!*

(JEREMIAH 9:21)

Redirected traffic and yellow police tape two blocks from my home told me that something serious had occurred earlier in the day. But not until the next day did I hear the details: A nineteen-year-old was gunned down, fled injured, and finally was destroyed by a bullet. His body lay uncovered on the street next to a car riddled with bullets. Just another story about violence in a Chicago neighborhood?

No.

This was a teenager murdered in broad daylight in *my* neighborhood. This was a teenager who had played on my church's junior high basketball team. I had never met him, had never heard his name—but I cried for him, for his family, for the neighborhood, for other kids making whatever choices got him killed.

I cried most of all for Ralph, a small fifth grader who is still—for now—in our church. Ralph admires gang members. And Ralph walked down the street to view the body.

What was going through his brain when he stood looking at that corpse? On which side of the gun did he mentally place himself? Did he cry? Or did his heart harden a little more?

Jesus wept over Jerusalem, crying out, "O Jerusalem, Jerusalem, the one who kills the prophets and stones those who are sent to her! How often I wanted to gather your children together, as a hen gathers her chicks under her wings, but you were not willing!" (Matthew 23:37). Does He cry over Chicago? I believe He does. Does He cry over your city?

Yes, God is sovereign. Yes, sin is man's rebellion against Him. But a merely academic approach to sin is inappropriate for a Christian. Adam and Eve never for a moment pictured that the results of their sin would include children shot to death by other children. That many of us have become numb to such stories is itself a travesty.

Today boys and girls are diagnosed with stress-related illnesses, and children are caring for themselves at younger and younger ages with less and less guidance from caring adults. Television, fashion-conscious peers, and drug-addicted musicians often try harder to influence children than parents do. Our children surely receive more stimulation than any other generation in history, and as a result even the most exciting entertainment bores them quickly. Adults don't feel they have much authority, so they make hesitant requests of children. Add the problems of single-parent families and pressure to use drugs or be sexually active, and you have a setting that pleads for loving Christians. Consider this:

> In 1950, adults (defined here as those over and including fifteen years of age) committed serious crimes at a rate 215 times that of the rate of child crime. By 1960, adults committed serious crimes at a rate 8 times that of child crime; by 1979, the rate was 5.5 times. . . . Between 1950 and 1979, the rate of adult crime increased threefold. The fast-closing difference between the rates of adult and child crime is almost wholly accounted for by a staggering rise in child crime. Between 1950 and 1979, the rate of serious crimes committed by children increased 11,000 percent![1]

Scripture says of Christ that He saw a large crowd and "was moved with compassion for them, because they were like sheep not having a shepherd. So He began to teach them many things" (Mark 6:34). Those last words caught my attention. We often don't link "compassion" and "teaching." Clearly, Jesus does. Teaching today demands compassion. And having compassion means being careful to teach rather than merely entertain, lest our children remain ignorant of Christ.

Many times as I get to know a child's needs, my heart softens toward him, and I know better *how* to teach him. A girl's defiance becomes less significant measured against knowledge of her sexual abuse and her desperate need to keep adults at arms' length until they prove trustworthy. A boy's inattention becomes more understandable when I know he eats only two meals a day and the last meal was ten hours ago. I try to celebrate children's victories and joys with them, whether the experience is a new sibling, cheerleading practice, piano recitals, or even barely passing a hard test.

Do you weep with and for your children? Have you entered their world? Even if the youngsters you teach live in middle class or affluent communities, their childhood is probably not a pretty, sentimental affair. And if the sidewalks around you are stained with children's blood, beg God that He will never allow your heart to be hardened or numbed to news stories that break His heart.

Note

1. Neil Postman, *The Disappearance of Childhood* (New York: Vintage, 1982, 1994), 134.

For Thought

1. Look through your local paper for news stories about events unfriendly to childhood. Train yourself to notice such stories and to reflect on how they affect your students.

2. Look at a list of your students' names. Go down it slowly, praying for each child as you think about the areas of his life where Satan may have a foothold.

11

THE WONDER
OF CHILDHOOD

*Assuredly, I say to you, whoever does not receive
the kingdom of God as a little child will by no
means enter it.*

(LUKE 18:17)

What did Jesus mean when He challenged His disciples to become like children? Children squirm, they don't know much, they have short attention spans, they laugh at inappropriate times, and they ask questions that have nothing to do with what the teacher is saying. What on earth could Jesus have meant when He told us to imitate them? Didn't we spend our whole childhood trying frantically to become adults?

Boys and girls can't understand deep theological truths, but in childish naïveté and trust, they pray for impossible things—and God answers, because He honors such faith. Adults are proud of their self-sufficiency; children eat and sleep because someone else provides the means. That, too, they accept by faith, rarely worrying whether their parents can continue to care for their needs. They have an almost intuitive sense of God's presence that allows them to link God with the rest of life more readily than adults, who put life into neat boxes. Johann Christoph Blumhardt says it this way:

> It is part of despising the little ones if we trust too little in their understanding and their sensitivity in matters of the spirit. Yet we could easily observe that the opposite is true. Children, especially in their personal relationship with Jesus, are even more receptive, yes, more understanding, than adults. For many adults are used to listening superficially, while little ones do not miss the smallest or most insignificant thing.[1]

Children learn more readily than adults do, which allows them to memorize a vast number of songs and verses that will guide them the rest of their lives. They love to sing, and spontaneous joy can burst forth in songs of praise. The Bible is brand-new to them. Its stories and truths arouse awe and thanksgiving—which should remind grown-ups of the appropriate response to God. They ask odd questions that open up fresh truths to any adults within earshot. They are explorers, learning about the world with delight. They are creative, and they can be generous. They usually don't hold grudges, and they readily accept forgiveness.

Affection from children is natural, uninhibited, and unaffected. It is given without regard to polite or socially expected responses. Ask a child if he wants a hug, and the answer may be a quick no. So when the hug is his idea, it comes from his heart. One time I was baby-sitting a toddler. A couple of times, he smiled a shy, tender smile and put his arm around me. Later, we were sitting on the floor playing. Suddenly, with no hesitation, he came over and put both arms around me. He lingered in my arms, then he settled down, cuddled next to me. It's easy to see why God appreciates the love of children!

Walter Wangerin said of childhood:

> Yet, when we were children we laughed without embarrassment. . . . When we were children we could gasp with delight at a sudden, beautiful thing, yearning to touch it. We didn't worry whether our notions of beauty were naive. We didn't pretend sophistication. . . . When we were children we accepted forgiveness completely. It truly did—when it was truly given—ease us and allow us to begin again. . . . Children can move to sorrow instantly and instantly to gladness again, yet feel both profoundly. This is the emotional nimbleness of those who have not sickened their feelings with self-analysis nor thickened their motives with ambition.[2]

In general, the littlest child does not hide his emotions in embarrassment. Often he does not care, really, what others think of him. He swaggers confidently beside Mom; as long as his parents meet his needs, he is content. He does not anticipate future needs but confidently asks his parents to meet needs he has now.

Ah, for more childish faith! "For even if we were so religious that the whole world talked about us, we still wouldn't get into God's Kingdom unless we became children."[3]

Notes

1. Johann Christoph Blumhardt and Christoph Friedrich Blumhardt, *Thoughts About Children* (Rifton, N.Y.: Plough, 1980), 20.
2. Walter Wangerin, *Little Lamb, Who Made Thee?* (New York: HarperCollins, 1993), 59–60.
3. Blumhardt and Blumhardt, *Thoughts About Children,* 30.

For Thought

1. What are two additional reasons that childhood is beautiful?

2. How do the traits of childhood protect children from the harsh facts of today's world? In what ways can you protect these precious traits for the good of the boys and girls you teach?

12

THE FAITH
OF A CHILD

*Faith comes by hearing, and hearing
by the word of God.*

(ROMANS 10:17)

I well remember when prayer became more than a ritual to me.

In seventh grade, I helped with the fours and fives department of children's church. The supervisor of children's church, Irene Malanowski, had won my fierce love with her simple attention and affection. Then my family left the church without warning, and I grieved. The person I was grieving wasn't dead—just inaccessible with no good-bye.

I cried myself to sleep night after night. I often ran from the school playground to the bathroom to hide in a stall and bawl. I daydreamed, imagining myself at that church again, imagining her calling me to tell me she missed me and loved me. Then I realized there was one thing I hadn't done: I hadn't prayed about my problem.

I started praying that I would see Mrs. Malanowski again. My family was trying to sell our house and move out of Phoenix, so I asked God to place my request in the "urgent" category. I believed fervently that somehow He would answer.

Irene and her husband lived in a suburb at the other side of town. I had never seen them outside of church, and we weren't going back to that church. But I imagined running into them at the grocery store, at the park during a family picnic, or any of a dozen other places. I continued to pray and to wonder what God would do in His answer. Every time we went somewhere, I half-expected to see her.

Then one Saturday a pickup truck stopped in front of our house. I recognized the couple who got out of it, but I didn't trust my voice. I put down the potato I was peeling and said quietly, "It looks like we have visitors."

Mom looked over my shoulder and announced what my mouth couldn't bring itself to say: "It's the Malanowskis."

It turned out that Mr. Malanowski was a real-estate agent with a practice around the corner. (I hadn't known that.) That Saturday he and his wife were out for a drive, and he decided for some reason to go by his office. He swung down our street, saw our For Sale sign, recognized the house as ours, and remembered a client who wanted a house in our area. So God used a whole series of "coincidences" to answer the faith of a young girl.

Mrs. Malanowski came in with her husband, I sidled up next to her, and she smiled at me and held out her hand so I could hold it.

Adults often get sidetracked from faith by the realities of life. We know how impossible a given prayer would be, so we don't ask it—and God instead shows His power to the child who naively, trustingly asks. A little child is awed by her daddy's power to grant wishes, so she brings her needs to him without any sense that she might inconvenience him. He's much bigger and stronger than she is, and he loves her. So she trusts him. And by finding him trustworthy, she learns to trust God.

Adults speak of God's transcendence (His standing above everything He has created) and immanence (voluntarily being close to His creation). We debate how both aspects could be true of God at the same time. Yet the child who does not know the words knows that although her daddy is much bigger than she is, she is important to him. His "transcendence" and "immanence" lead her to God.

Some children don't know their fathers. Some fathers are distracted, disinterested, or abusive. Yet even the children of such fathers have the mental image of what a good father is like. A child with a loving father learns faith easier, but almost any child comes to God with more faith than we sophisticated grown-ups use. Jesus pointed that out (Matthew 18), and He reminded His followers that adults only *think* they are self-sufficient. He told them, "Without Me you can do nothing" (John 15:5).

Ten-year-old Melissa told me about accepting the Lord. She told me only because the children's pastor encouraged her to, and she told me reluctantly and quickly: "I'm a Christian." No, she didn't want to tell me about it. Why not? "I don't want to be a Christian." Why not? "Because I'm scared." Although Melissa needed to move past the fear of being a Christian, I saw that she understood the seriousness of the step she had taken. She knew that a relationship with God was not a light thing.

God is not a distracted father. The Christian does not need to fear His neglect or His irrational anger. Our Father longs to hear the prayers of His children of all ages. What are you afraid to ask Him? How can you encourage the faith of children in your class?

For Thought

1. Which situations in your classroom seem impossible? Pray that God will grant you faith, wisdom, patience, and love for the children or parents or church leaders involved.

2. What child in your class faces a situation that seems unfixable? What are you and/or the child praying for in the situation?

13

KNOWING THE CHARACTERISTICS OF AGE GROUPS

Train up a child in the way he should go, and when he is old he will not depart from it.

(PROVERBS 22:6)

Teachers need to have some idea of what to expect from most students of a given age. I have taken worksheets to class that were too great a struggle for kids not quite old enough for them. I've had kids ask what some word means after I'd carelessly left it undefined. And I've seen kids bored because they were not being challenged enough.

If you have been teaching awhile, you have probably noticed that over the past few years age-group distinctions have changed dramatically in two ways: Boys and girls are worldly-wise earlier, yet they are slower at taking responsibility and growing up. What other facts are true of them? Below are some characteristics generally true of children in a particular age bracket, along with a few ways those characteristics should affect how you teach them.

Kindergarten and first grade. These two grades are separated in most church programs. In my church, they are together, which seems to work better than having first-graders with second and third graders. Kindergarten and first grade (ages five to seven) are primarily the grades for learning basic reading skills. These children are usually affectionate, trusting, and eager to please.

Avoid activities that require reading. You can help kids memorize by having them repeat short phrases after you. Use hands-on activities, but don't expect a lot of manual dexterity, and don't use complicated projects. "Discipline problems" are often just children who aren't used to sitting still; problems can be largely eliminated by allowing kids to move about. Teach with stories and very concrete examples. Encourage imagination and acting out the story.

Second and third grade. These children are beginning to master reading. They do not understand figurative or symbolic language. They have a sense of wonder about the world, and they are interested in learning about God and personal faith. They like belonging to a group.

They often enjoy working together on projects rather than separately, although some children of this age can be quite competitive. They learn best with stories, but they enjoy reading simple passages from the Bible. They like drawing and making simple projects.

Fourth and fifth grade. These students—juniors—are facing issues that used to wait until high school or at least junior high. Some talk about dating or show high levels of interest in sex. They are quite aware of fashion trends and music. They know about drugs and gangs. Although juniors are probably not yet directly tempted by them, the teacher cannot afford to be naive. These are no longer little children. They are developing opinions. They love exploring and learning about subjects that interest them. Children of this age enjoy life, and boys and girls are beginning to develop different interests. Some girls have entered puberty. Boys are considerably more macho in groups, particularly in the presence of girls, than alone.

It is possible to go into a subject in depth, but wide variance in learning ability requires sensitivity: Don't ask slow readers to read aloud if they will be embarrassed by such attention. Children of this age have great capacity for memorization. Male role models are crucial, as boys are beginning to define what masculinity means, and some may resist the guidance of women.

Sixth grade. Sixth grade is sometimes lumped with juniors, sometimes with junior high. Ideally, your church puts them with the same group in which local schools place sixth graders. Many of these kids are feeling insecure. They don't feel they belong in "the in group" at school, some may already be aware of the pressures they will face in upcoming years, and they are sensitive to the failures of adults around them. They are beginning to grasp symbolic or figurative concepts. They are hero worshipers. They are ambivalent about the opposite sex; girls are obsessed with talking about boys but shy and giggly in their presence. Strong group ties begin to form, and they may have mood swings.

One of the greatest challenges for the teacher will be bridging the gap between untaught children and those who have grown up in church. Look for practical ways for the second category of kids to be involved in service to the church. Sixth graders are in many ways almost on an adult level of understanding, so don't baby them.

Seventh and eighth grade. Junior high is a time of change. Students show increasing interest in the outside world and are willing to be involved in needs they see. It's often a time of great insecurity and high levels of peer pressure. Sexual activity, drug and alcohol use, and gang attachment all skyrocket during junior high years, although levels are still much lower than in high school. Many seventh and eighth graders are willing to form firm attachments with one particular adult who pays attention to them.

I am concerned that many junior high ministries begin to pay more attention to social aspects of teaching (making kids feel a part of the group) than they do to actually teaching them the Bible. Many teachers use methods based on how much they will interest kids without considering very critically whether those methods are appropriate for teaching them about God. If you teach this age group, challenge them; don't just do what everyone else does.

More important than knowing general characteristics, however, is knowing your own students. There are numerous ways to get to know more about the world they live in: Subscribe for a year to a magazine geared to their age.[1] Occasionally, watch the television shows they watch. Talk to a teacher who works with the age group full-time. Notice the vocabulary level your Sunday school curriculum uses, and pay attention to the kinds of stories it uses to illustrate the lessons. You also can sit down with children one-on-one and ask them some good questions about what they like to do.

Note

1. Focus on the Family publishes several child-level magazines for various ages. On the secular side, Cricket Magazine Group produces high-quality magazines for various ages.

For Further Study

1. Read a book or an article that focuses on teaching children of the age group you work with. Your teacher's guide may be a good starting place.

2. When you aren't responsible for teaching the lesson, take a week to observe your class. It might help to discreetly take notes. What do the children talk about? What is their vocabulary level? What are their interests? How do they interact with each other?

14

IS IT SIN OR IMMATURITY?

*When I was a child, I spoke as a child, I
understood as a child, I thought as a child.*

(1 CORINTHIANS 13:11)

During the lesson on Jesus facing down Satan's temptations, I asked my class of first and second graders to tell me things Satan might tempt them to do. One child suggested "fall asleep in church." I said, "That could be Satan, but it's probably just because you're sleepy." If Jesus acknowledged His disciples' weak flesh when those adults fell asleep rather than praying with Him, I think we can permit bodily weakness from six- and seven-year-olds.

Later in the day I taught the same lesson to third and fourth graders. Applying the lesson in a small-group time, I pointed out that some temptations rise from our own sinful nature and some are temptations from Satan. Just then my assistant chastised two girls, saying, "See, Satan is making you do that, just like she was saying." Since their misbehavior had not caught my attention, I looked to see what they were doing. What was this demonically influenced misbehavior? Rustling Bible pages. Again, the issue was not true misbehavior, just childish wiggling that could have been quieted by silently calling attention to it.

When dealing with childish distractions, it helps to start by determining which category the behavior fits:

1. sin (rebellion, intentional misbehavior, disobedience)
2. inappropriate behavior stemming from immaturity (going against social or cultural acceptable behavior, distracting other children, or behaving rudely)
3. acceptable childishness (minor wiggling or other conduct that doesn't distract other children)

I frequently encounter two or three boys wrestling in the church lobby. I don't consider that an appropriate activity in the church building, and some unsuspecting elderly person could be tripped by their rambunctiousness. But it's not sin. When I find boys wrestling, I simply get their attention and tell them calmly, "This isn't the place for that. Go outside if you want to wrestle."

If a little girl pulls a small stuffed animal out of her pocket and pets it during the lesson, once again that's not sin—but it is distracting to her and to others. I tell her to put it back in her pocket and leave it there. It only becomes a problem if temptation overwhelms her and she disobeys by taking it out again. In such cases, I confiscate the toy until the end of the class period. Part of our responsibility as teachers is to socialize children, but it's important to distinguish "be nice" from the Gospel.

I like Walter Wangerin's definition of discipline, which distinguishes between punishment that occurs because some action angered an adult and careful correction because the child needs to be taught appropriate behavior. He says, "Discipline is an extended and carefully managed event, not a sudden, spontaneous, personal reaction to the child's behavior."[1]

Unless the misbehavior is deliberate and defiant, discipline can usually be gentle redirection: a preventive hand on the shoulder to get a child's attention, accompanied by either a small smile or a serious warning look, as appropriate; a whispered reminder of a forgotten rule; a suggestion of something more productive the child can do. If you are not the one up front teaching, merely moving to sit next to a noisy child may keep him quiet, and it puts you next to him to provide guidance with less distraction to other children. Sometimes it's necessary for an assistant to take an unruly child outside the classroom and talk with him where he can't distract the other boys and girls.

Separating two children who are diverting each other's attention often helps, and forbidding them to sit next to each other at all can help with chronic misbehavior. They can earn the privilege of sitting next to each other again rather than seeing it as a right.

Part of training children is also encouraging positive behavior. You can give a timid girl confidence to try something when she hesitates, then show enthusiasm over her success or even her courage to try. You can shower attention on the boy who usually misbehaves to get attention but who is showing great self-control today. Try complimenting him to another adult in front of him. With caution, you can even give a quick compliment to a child in front of his peers.

Recently I smiled to myself, remembering my own early days working with children, as I saw a group of junior-high assistants in a class. Eager to give commands, they watched every move the children made: "No, put your foot over there. Quit wiggling. Sit up straight." They were clearly proud to have the authority of adults. But with greater maturity and experience comes a better sense of whether something is just childishness, immaturity that needs to be gently corrected, or sin that demands loving intervention.

Note

1. Walter Wangerin, *Little Lamb, Who Made Thee?* (New York: HarperCollins, 1993), 69.

For Evaluation

1. Watch your class this week, and gauge your reactions to children's misbehavior. Do you move in too quickly to punish mere childishness? Do you let distracting misbehavior continue?

2. Watch other teachers or helpers in your class or other classes. How do they maintain discipline? Is their discipline effective? Why or why not?

15

THE PROBLEM WITH SELF-ESTEEM

He must increase, but I must decrease.

(JOHN 3:30)

But know this, that in the last days perilous times will come: For men will be lovers of themselves . . . haughty, lovers of pleasure rather than lovers of God.

(2 TIMOTHY 3:1-2, 4)

One day I sat in on a girls' Sunday school class and listened. The leader asked for strong points kids their age might have, and the girls volunteered what they believed their strengths were: "I'm good at math." "I'm really good at keeping secrets." After they made the list, the leader went through it item by item and asked, "OK, how many of you are good at . . .?" Although the list varied widely, from math, drawing, reading, and sports to being kind to others and keeping secrets, either all the girls raised their hands or all but one did for each category. I said to myself, *Yes, we do have a self-esteem problem with this generation!*

Christian education literature has picked up the mantra that secular wisdom has been repeating for years: Children need to learn self-esteem. The idea can be convincing. Some children come to class with sad, averted eyes. Today's children are often lonely, loaded with adult-sized burdens that seem to require an adult-sized sense of confidence rather than a child's fragility—and certainly not the sensitivities of a timid child.

But is "healthy self-esteem" the answer? Is a confident but unskilled and unloved person really in a better position, or is he just deceived? It seems to me that this generation of adults has realized how much easier it is to encourage a child to have self-confidence than to build confidence the old-fashioned way: by encouraging and loving a child as he goes through the hard work of learning genuine knowledge and gaining real skills. Discovering the truth that one's self-worth has been built on nothing but confident talk can lead to a tragic loss of hope. In today's world, the person without hope is vulnerable to drugs, gangs, even suicide. But he is not better qualified to make sense of his world.

And, contrary to most of what we are told today, the child who actually believes the hype and develops a strong sense of "self-esteem" is set up for a fall of a different kind.

Much of what the modern world calls self-esteem is nothing more than what the Bible talks about as the sin of pride. William Kilpatrick says,

> Being completely self-accepting is not exactly a formula for responsible behavior. Some of recent history's worst scoundrels—Joseph Stalin, Idi Amin, Saddam Hussein, Manuel Noriega—seem to have been quite self-satisfied. The trouble with such people is not that they lack self-esteem but that they feel themselves accountable to no outside law or standard. It's not even necessary to consult history books. Any pimp, con artist, or drug pusher will prove the point. As a rule, they enjoy what they do and seem to have few, if any, self-doubts.[1]

The young girl on the TV program cried as she talked to her camp counselor. Nobody loved her, she felt worthless, and she wasn't sure if life was worth living. The counselor listened compassionately, then she told the girl, "You need to learn to love yourself." I should have expected that answer; modern books (some of them Christian) encourage that response. But it turned a knife inside me, and I wanted to yell at the screen: "No, don't tell her that! That isn't going to help. Please, please, tell her, '*I* love you.'"

We are told that until we love ourselves, we won't be able to love others. Some Christians have even said Jesus meant that when He said, "You shall love your neighbor as yourself." But I want to suggest that self-love and self-esteem are only the desperate answers of a desperately dysfunctional culture. It's not by loving oneself that one is freed to love others. *It's by being loved.*

Teacher, love your students. More important, make sure they know your love is but a dim reflection of God's love for them. Our value comes from our being made in His image and being loved by Him. Encourage them for their good qualities so they can have confidence that is well-grounded. Teach them in areas where they need to learn more. Help them understand that self-centeredness and pride are sins, and help them learn to love others while you love them. Then you can in good conscience ignore what our culture says about self-esteem.

> Whereas the public school "self-esteem" programs teach young people that they are special by encouraging them to look inward, we teach them their uniqueness by helping them to look upward to God's call and then outward in mission.[2]

Notes

1. William Kilpatrick, *Why Johnny Can't Tell Right from Wrong and What We Can Do About It* (New York: Touchstone, 1992), 41–42.
2. Marva J. Dawn, *Is It a Lost Cause? Having the Heart of God for the Church's Children* (Grand Rapids: Eerdmans, 1997), 229.

For Evaluation

1. Which children in your class seem particularly insecure or withdrawn? How have you shown love to these kids?

2. Next time you teach, notice how the needy children respond to you. Is it with fear or averted eyes, with clinging, or some other way? What can you do or say to show those children you love them?

16

WHEN THEY ARE WEAK

*God has chosen the foolish things of the
world to put to shame the wise, and God
has chosen the weak things of the world to
put to shame the things which are mighty;
. . . that no flesh should glory in His
presence.*

(1 CORINTHIANS 1:27, 29)

Five-year-old Brian looked innocent enough: white uncombed hair arranged over a plump face and a short stocky figure. His conversation hinted at learning problems: "Me want to do that."

Was this the same boy with penetrating, hard eyes, a cheek full of chewing tobacco, and—if the children's whispers were to be believed—the foulest mouth on the school bus? The other children in my Bible club were uncomfortable around a kindergartner who talked the way he did. Several of them whispered to me, "You should hear the things Brian says on the bus! My mother told me to stay away from him."

When I mentioned Brian to Mary, the gentle seventy-three-year-old woman across the street from him, she told me, "That boy is no good! The managers should kick his family out." Neighborhood boys had smashed religious figures in Mary's yard. She said Brian was the leader.

The dirt bike propped outside the mobile-home court's clubhouse, where the Bible club met every Thursday afternoon, reminded me of that rumored tough side of Brian. So did the tobacco can in his pocket and the children's whispers and glances in his direction. But Brian himself, the white-haired little boy in front of me, eager to be there and one of the best behaved boys in the bunch, contradicted the rumors and forced me to rethink what I thought I knew about teaching.

It didn't matter how many times I went over the Bible verse with him, word by word. It didn't matter what incentives I gave him to learn, how much I encouraged him. After repeating two words, Brian looked up frustrated and said, "Me can't learn it." But Brian didn't worry what others thought about him. It didn't bother him that many weeks he was the only child who did not learn the Bible verse. He didn't stop coming to the club because he decided he was not getting much out of it.

Each Thursday afternoon for two years, I led a train of children ages three to twelve down every street in my mother's mobile-home court and knocked on each door of the club's members. Sometimes nobody came; sometimes eight or ten did. Often Brian was not home when we stopped by his house. When he was home, he was usually just about to jump on his dirt bike, or he was in the back of the family pickup, ready to go to the store. Whatever he was doing, he quickly changed his mind and ran to find his parents. "Me go Bible club." The dirt bike and Brian joined our train. When Brian couldn't decide which of two things he'd rather do, his teenage brother Kevin encouraged him, "Go to the Bible club."

The teenager, about sixteen, seemed strangely innocent compared to his tobacco-chewing little brother. He dressed well, looked me in the eye, talked to me politely, and seemed to show maturity in his interest in Brian's welfare. The boys' parents were lower middle class, apparently kind parents who loved their children. I wanted to sit down with them, to ask why they were supporting my efforts with their son. I wanted to ask why a kindergarten child was chewing tobacco, where he learned his bad language. But I was a timid teenager, and I didn't.

How much did my lessons influence Brian? Why did he come so eagerly? I prayed for time with him—without his friend Justin, without the dirt bikes. One day none of the children who formed the train were home when I wound through. I went to the clubhouse anyway and sat. Twenty minutes later, I gathered my supplies and got ready to go. Before I could leave, Brian burst in, panting.

I was unsure how to respond to this answer to prayer. Brian sat, waiting for me to teach him. I sat, unsure how to do it. Not sure what he needed, what he would understand. I pulled out my "Wordless Book" (an evangelistic booklet popularized by Child Evangelism Fellowship) and went through it, using simple language. I didn't know what level of understanding I should aim for. I was teaching a five-year-old with a three-year-old's language skills, yet Brian could clearly keep up with others his age socially.

After the short lesson, I took paper and crayons from the bag that also held the more complicated project I'd intended the class to do that day. "Brian, do you want to draw a picture about Jesus?"

What he drew looked to me like random scribblings, but when he told me he was finished, I asked him to tell me about his picture. He pointed to the center of the purple scratches and explained, "That's a cross." He moved his finger a little to trace a different scribble. "That's Jesus on the cross."

"What did Jesus do on the cross?"

"He died."

"Why did He die?"

Brian shrugged. So I explained the Gospel, again, using simple language and praying silently. Then we chatted for a while before I dismissed him.

Too often I've forgotten the meaning of some of the best-known words in Christianity: "They are weak, but He is strong." I try to be strong, in control. Brian was weak, vulnerable. But this little boy had the simplicity of an understanding not cluttered by misunderstood doctrine, doubt, and pride. He did not know as much about the Bible as I did—indeed he did not even know my Savior yet—but what he did know was not crowded out by the determination to look strong. I still pray for this little boy, now a young man, who would not give up just because he did not learn at the speed of the other children. And I still wonder what he learned from his years of attending my little Bible club.

For Thought

1. Do you have a child who just does not seem to understand or who seems never to listen or even try to understand? Pray for, and look for, an opportunity for one-on-one contact with the child.

2. Have you gone through the Gospel in your class lately? Would your children be able to explain why Jesus died? Do they know that their own good works cannot earn them favor with God?

PART 3

RELATING TO CHILDREN

Dear, supernal Parent, God of my children, save them! . . .
Protect them against the enemies that would kill them. But if they
must suffer storms or treachery, turn their suffering to advantage—
that it always turn them back to you again. . . .
Make my children humble. Let hurting cause in them a genuine
humility. And let their transgressions cause no more harm than a
personal hurt—for I know them. They will sin. . . . Let their
repentance find your forgiveness and seize them thereby and hold
them close unto your bosom forever and ever.
Save them from the world and from themselves. Amen.
I love them, sweet Jesus. Amen.

—WALTER WANGERIN,
Little Lamb, Who Made Thee?
(New York: HarperCollins, 1993), 159–60.

17

PIGGYBACK RIDES AND OTHER ACTS OF LOVE

*And Jesus, when He came out, saw a great
multitude and was moved with compassion for
them, because they were like sheep not having a
shepherd. So He began to teach them many things.*

(MARK 6:34)

I had just turned seven, and I had never been to camp before. One of the teenage boys, George, talked to me on the bus on the way to camp. The second day I saw him again at supper. I'd never noticed him much at church, but now when he saw me and winked, I felt shy.

Halfway through the meal, teenagers started singing loudly, "Get your elbows off the table, dear George . . ." Everyone was looking at George. I quickly made sure my elbows weren't on the table so they wouldn't all look at me. The second verse offered George's "punishment": "Round the building you must go, you must go, you must go. Round the building you must go—with a girl."

George got up bravely and stood in the doorway. When they finished singing, he looked at me, smiled, and motioned for me to come. I ran to him, and he asked, "Do you want a piggyback ride?" I nodded, he boosted me onto his shoulders, and away we went around the building—twice. From my high altitude, I looked in the windows of the dining hall. I was proud to be in on the joke with George. I felt his strong shoulders under me, and I put my chin on the top of his head. More than twenty-five years later, I still feel the joy of that encounter. Somebody noticed me and made me feel special.

My older brother Ed was sixteen when he went to Bible college, and I was five. He came to visit me at school when I was in first grade, and I was extra proud to show my big brother—the one who was in *college*—around my grade school. I was even more proud to see that he still carried in his wallet a picture of a smiling, freckled brunette in a pink dress: my kindergarten portrait. I've always liked that particular picture because Ed loved me enough to carry it.

Irene Malanowski knew me when I was in seventh grade. I saw her for only about five minutes each Sunday, and I don't remember a single conversation we had. I do remember that she smiled when she saw me, that she put her arm around me even when my deodorant wasn't working, and that she talked to me as if I was someone important to her. Those little bits of love were strong enough to a desperately lonely junior high student that I vowed to name my first daughter Irene.

Often teachers look for conspicuous evidence that their teaching is changing lives or that their students feel loved. Yet few important things in life are as showy as fireworks. In teaching, it is often the little things, done consistently and lovingly, that reach children who need your love and God's.

I'm often awkward with a child one-on-one, particularly over the phone. Kids are usually poor conversationalists. They don't suggest topics when the conversation falters, and they often answer questions with the briefest of answers ("yes," "no," "I guess"), leaving the adult scrambling to come up with something to keep the conversation going. Add to that the "generation gap"—the different interests of the two and the strong awareness of both parties of the age difference—and the awkwardness is usually felt by both. But it helps to recognize that that very fact gives you something in common. You are two awkward people who are trying not to be awkward and who are trying to communicate. Your job is to bring yourself to the child's level without condescension and to keep the conversation going as smoothly as possible.

A child isn't looking for you to have perfect conversation skills or perfect ability to communicate on his level; he is looking for you to care enough to give your best effort and talk with him. Pulling out puppets or doing some activity together often makes it easier for a child to talk. A girl puppet held by a ten-year-old girl once told the daddy puppet I was holding that she'd had a bad day at school; kids had made fun of her because she loves God. Our two puppets spent twenty minutes discussing that scenario. Although ordinarily I avoid having a puppet (a make-believe object) talk about God, I had brought out the puppets because it seemed she had something she needed to talk about but couldn't bring up. After a few minutes of playing with animal puppets, she chose human puppets, and we had our discussion.

Some of your children may be desperate for the love of an adult. Some of those may squirm away from your touch, avoid eye contact, or even ignore you altogether. You may never know which of your students most need your love, and you may never know which of your small gestures will break into a wary heart or encourage a child who is struggling.

A sentence I heard in passing has stuck with me: "Every kid needs at least one person who's crazy about him." Do you have at least one child you're "crazy about"?

For Thought

1. Do you have one or two children or teenagers who seem to be drawn to you or to whom you feel a particular bond?

2. How can you say "I care about you" to these children? From what you have seen of them, how would you rank their need for love?

18

LEARNING HUMILITY AND PATIENCE

But the fruit of the Spirit is love, joy, peace,
longsuffering, kindness, goodness, faithfulness,
gentleness, self-control. Against such there
is no law.

(GALATIANS 5:22–23)

The first several months I taught Rachel, she tested every rule. If she climbed on a table and I told her to get down, she jumped to another one. If I told her not to touch some fragile item, she picked it up. Rachel bounced, pulled things off shelves, laughed, and seemed to ignore my words.

But from Rachel I learned something about patience that surprised me: It's not automatic. I always thought some people were patient and others were not. I did think impatient people could learn to be patient, and I noticed that patience was a fruit of the Spirit. Yet mentally I graded people as "patient" or "impatient" just as I might decide whether or not someone was naturally athletic.

I find it an encouraging truth that patience is a choice. When a child tests me, shows disrespect, or disobeys, patience does not come naturally. But what I *know* can fill my mind and cancel out how I *feel*. What I know includes the love Jesus has for children, their need for salvation, and the fact that children need to be taught how to behave. If *I* did not just absorb everything, why should I expect them to?

I also recognize the apathetic way many of today's parents are rearing their children and the fact that many boys and girls live with only one parent—or neither one. Rachel is a foster child who has not had many consistent adults in her life, and therefore she feels a strong need to test an adult's love before she dares trust herself to it. But the pictures with a written "I love you" and the tight hugs that I got from Rachel in later years reinforced my earlier decision to love her consistently even when I didn't feel like it.

Many children have little to no contact with unhurried adults. Both parents work, or the kids live with one parent who works and they are occasionally shuttled off to the other parent. Children's own schedules are often crammed with sporting events, private lessons, and other time fillers, not to mention homework. Sometimes misbehavior can be their only way to say to an adult, "Slow down and give me your attention. I need you."

Teaching is not something that can be done in a hurry. When a child's behavior demands discipline, calm yourself and address the child. Patient, fair discipline will gain far more for interpersonal relationships and class structure than will quick "fixing" of a behavior problem.

But few of us are naturally patient. For this trait, we need to lean hard on the Holy Spirit.

I had many opportunities in the classroom to reinforce what I was trying to teach Rachel. One night I had to deal with a scuffle between her and one of the boys on the way down to the gym. They apologized as required, although somewhat insincerely.

Later, as the girls finished getting drinks at the drinking fountain, Rachel jumped to the end of the line to get a second one. I let her drink for a few seconds, then told her it was time to go. I spoke to her several times, and she continued to ignore me, probably drinking more than she would have otherwise. So when she finally came to the stairs, I told her she was on time-out when we got to the project room. Time-out is the method of discipline that our club program was using in such instances.

When we got to the room, I pulled a chair aside for Rachel. She sat in it, but she turned her back to me and faced the wall. I said, "Let me know when you're ready to talk to me," and I walked away. I glanced back later, and she was still facing the wall. The next time I looked, she motioned me over, so I went and sat beside her. I asked, "Do you know why I had to punish you?" She turned her back again, though not as decisively.

I put my arm around her and explained the problem. Then I told her, "You need to learn how to obey, and I'm going to help you learn that. Can you think of any other ways I can help you learn that?" She shook her head quickly, and I hid the urge to smile.

When I told her which actions had been inappropriate, she said, "I'm sorry," and when I told her to look at me, she did so. I released her, praying that she had learned something. I suspect the punishment strengthened her desire to obey. She needed to have me pass the tests she had set up before I could earn her respect, and I needed to be a consistent part of her life so that she could trust me in the process. Although the testing lasted a few more months, that day was a decisive one and further encounters with her were easier.

For Thought

1. Think back to your own childhood. Were the adults around you—parents, teachers, relatives, neighbors—generally patient? By their words and example did they teach you patience or impatience?

2. In what situations do you find patience difficult? You might find it useful to ask someone to hold you accountable in this area.

19

RESPECTING CHILDREN

But whoever causes one of these little ones
who believe in Me to sin, it would be
better for him if a millstone were hung
around his neck, and he were drowned in
the depth of the sea.

(MATTHEW 18:6)

Imagine this scenario. At prayer meeting, the leader breaks the large group into smaller clusters of three or four people with their chairs gathered into little circles. Someone in your group starts to tell a long story you've heard before, so your attention wanders. When your name is mentioned in a neighboring circle, your ears perk up. It's your Sunday school teacher who has just mentioned you, so you lean over to hear what he is saying.

"Yeah," he says, "but she keeps committing this same sin. We really need to pray for her, because she . . ." Have you overheard enough to be mad yet? Something within you reacts against mentioning someone's sins as a prayer request—especially when it's *your* sins that are being discussed.

Have you ever done something similar to the children you teach? Does getting together to pray with other teachers mean you discuss particular children and name their specific sins? It seems different somehow to discuss *children's* flaws and misdeeds publicly, but should it?

How does a teacher deal with these questions? Here's my personal answer: I won't discuss or pray for a child by name unless (a) I know that other adults present already know the issues involved because of their own experience with that child, or (b) every other person present needs to know of the child's behavior because of the relationship he has to the child (my supervisor in the program, my teaching partner, the child's parents).

Part of respecting a person is taking him seriously. So when a child cries over a "broken heart," it may seem cute, but it's not funny. And the child will undoubtedly respect the adult who takes the hurt seriously more than the adult who responds with amusement. A child who is trying really hard to do something and ends up making messy blunders may stir up amusement in an adult, but the child's efforts need to be taken seriously, as well.

I find children cute. Their charm, affection, and other endearing qualities are a large part of the reason I enjoy being around them. But I rarely *show* them that I think they're cute. Boys and girls over preschool age are usually frustrated by that reaction from adults—they do not consider themselves to be *little* children anymore.

Many adults, particularly women, are also guilty of laughing or smiling when a child misbehaves. It may be hard not to laugh when an eight-month-old hits a toddler over the head with a toy. The act is not deliberate, and the scene can be quite comical. But laughter encourages the "culprit" to do it on purpose next time, and it tells the child who has been hit that you don't care.

Most often when we talk about respect between adults and children, the discussion assumes only one direction for that respect. We teach children Ephesians 6:1 to encourage their obedience, yet we fail to read a mere three verses beyond that. Verse 4 is written to fathers but relevant to all who work with children: "Do not provoke your children to wrath, but bring them up in the training and admonition of the Lord."

What does "do not provoke" mean? Don't make a child *righteously* angry. A child has a right to expect a certain standard of behavior from those who attempt to lead him. By "expect," I do not mean the demands of a spoiled child; I mean a child's unconscious, reasonable assumptions. He can expect that you yourself will follow the commands you teach to him. He can expect that you will take his fears and joys seriously. He can expect you to protect him from physical and emotional harm. And he can expect you to respond to him as a person made in the image of God. Demanding obedience without offering protection is but one act of disrespect. Demanding respect without being worthy of it is another. Unworthiness could mean hypocritical moral conduct, abusive behavior, or any number of other things.

Respect is a significant element of adult/child interaction. I'd like to suggest that the main work should be yours. Look less at whether or not the children you teach respect you and more at whether you have earned their respect. Ideally, they should be able to offer you respect readily because you respect them and you are respectable. I believe that is the most ideal situation for parents or teachers. Tom Locke pointed out,

> Gangs are willing to recognize young people's gifts and contribution. Gangs will let a ten-year-old join, let a thirteen-year-old have rank and "call shots." A sixteen-year-old can run a whole community. While we are telling kids to shut up, gangs are making them leaders.[1]

Sometimes earning respect is hard work. A few years ago a young inner-city boy was placed in my class in the middle of the year. His attitude toward me clearly said, "You can't teach me anything, because you can't possibly understand me." I proceeded carefully with him, allowing male leaders to deal with him as much as possible until I had earned his respect. Sometimes children feel cornered by adults, and when they fight back, both parties lose. I didn't want any unnecessary confrontation that would encourage open defiance. I did have to confront his behavior once, and fortunately another leader backed me up in a way that continued to assert my own authority. Eventually I saw his defenses against me go down, and I was able to deal with him on a deeper level. But first I had to earn his respect, which took patience, respect on my part, gentle firmness, and prayer.

Note

1. Tom Locke, "Reaching Youth Involved in Gangs," in *A Heart for the City: Effective Ministries to the Urban Community*, ed. John Fuder (Chicago: Moody, 1999), 440.

For Evaluation

1. Think through the way you talk to others about your class's discipline problems. Is it respectful and honoring?

2. What is one aspect of your life that may make it difficult for children to respect you?

20

TEACHING CHILDREN RESPECT

*Obey those who rule over you, and
be submissive, for they watch out for
your souls, as those who must give
account. Let them do so with joy and
not with grief, for that would be
unprofitable for you.*

(HEBREWS 13:17)

Your class has functioned smoothly for months. The kids like you, and they respect you. You know each child by name, you know where they stand spiritually, you know their interests, and you even know what is likely to offend or annoy them. They enjoy the class, and most of them seem to be learning. One kid you don't even know ran up to you last month to say she can't wait until next year when she gets to be in your class.

Then Robert's family moves into the neighborhood, and Robert arrives in your class. His scowl is included at no extra charge. When your best student answers a question, Robert mumbles something to the smart kid that you hope you didn't hear right. When you look at Robert, he slowly, deliberately, dumps the girl in the chair in front of him onto the floor.

What do you do? If you read the previous chapter, you may think that's a trick question. "Well, I work hard to earn his respect, of course." Right . . . and wrong. His respect applies only indirectly right now. His obedience, and the safety and order of your class, apply very directly.

Ideally, a child will honor you because you have earned his respect. But one step in earning a child's respect may be demanding his obedience and not backing down when he tests you to see if you mean it. Some children won't happen to like you, or they're not in the mood to listen, or their parents usually make suggestions rather than give commands, so they see respect as optional. For all these scenarios, the next level of respect is appropriate: commanded respect.

"Robert, I know you don't want to sit in that seat, but I didn't ask you if you wanted to. I *told* you to sit there and be quiet. You haven't earned the right to sit wherever you want. So sit down and be quiet." The command is given respectfully, but it is said in a tone that says you expect to be obeyed.

Beginning teachers usually make the mistake of starting too gently in matters of discipline. That may be because of a sentimental notion of children (if I love them, they'll love me back, and they'll be sweet little dolls). It may be because of fear that the children won't obey anyway, and that firmness will just make it worse, because they'll laugh. It may be due to an honest belief that classrooms with less discipline are more fun.

How to discipline is best learned gradually, through experience of what works and what does not, rather than through theory. It's unpleasant to be the sole disciplinarian in a rowdy class when you're just learning how to teach. But whether you get to learn slowly or must learn fast, let me tell you a secret: The teacher who has order in the classroom will gain more respect than the teacher who does not.

Remember those helpless substitute teachers when you were in junior high? When the class was in chaos, did your classmates whisper how much they admired the teacher . . . or did they say other kinds of things? Many students disdain teachers who cannot keep order. If you are a weak disciplinarian, you might want to sit in on the class of a teacher who has a reputation for being beloved by her students and see how she enforces discipline.

I'm not pretending that students will swarm all over you with hugs because you keep order. They might. They might not. That's not the best evaluation of a good teacher. I am saying that the structured classroom feels safer for children. It's easier on their nerves as well as on your own. Being adored is not an essential part of your task. Being effective is. Harshness is counterproductive, but firmness is basic.

The child who tests you should never have the option to disobey. If you ignore or give in to direct disobedience, you and the child have both lost, and the battle will be harder next time. Put as much energy into the first confrontation as you need to. That energy should be verbal as much as possible, and it should be in a controlled tone of voice rather than screaming or threatening. You may need to take a child's arm or put your hand on his shoulder. But do not push, hit, or otherwise hurt a child, and do not even touch him if you are too angry to do so rationally. Continue to engage the child until he obeys, or bring in another adult to reinforce your discipline. Future encounters with that child should then reinforce an expectation of quicker obedience.

If you sense that a child will be defiant beyond your ability to handle a problem, it may be better to tell him that you will deal with him later, then ignore his behavior until another adult is available to deal with him or you have an opportunity to speak with him alone. If you begin discipline and the child resists, *never* let him win, even if you must end the confrontation without firm closure but with the declaration of what you will do next: talk to his parents, restrict him from an activity the class is doing later, and so on. But make sure it does not become a battle of the wills in which you descend to his level. The child must not see the confrontation as a fight but as an issue where he's being disobedient. Do not back him into a corner so that his dignity forces him to fight you unnecessarily.

A big part of discipline is avoiding problems that have not yet happened. At a camp for juniors, I was helping guard the jail during a game of Capture the Flag. The prisoners were talking about an escape, which was against the rules. Noting that they had been kept confined to the limits of their endurance, I found the leader of the game and requested that she call an official jail break so that the children could be freed without the sin of open dis-obedience.

The next time Robert seeks to interrupt your class, how will you deal with the distrac-tion?

For Action

1. Think for a moment about your most difficult child. Write down two strengths you be-lieve he has. Write down two areas in which to pray for him. Pray for him.

2. Write the child a short letter or a postcard, or call him. When you see him in class, make an effort to greet him warmly before he has a chance to do something that requires disci-pline.

21

BEING THE ADULT IN THE CLASSROOM

*When I was a child, I spoke as a child, I
understood as a child, I thought as a child;
but when I became a man, I put away
childish things.*

(1 CORINTHIANS 13:11)

When I was fifteen and a somewhat new Sunday school teacher, a child in my class commented that Jesus was crucified on Friday. I had been taught that the crucifixion probably took place Wednesday or Thursday, so after class I "corrected" him. He told me his mother said it happened Friday, and I told him reasons it couldn't have been on Friday.

I look back on that immature confrontation with some embarrassment. I have since learned a few things about teaching and a few more about respecting my students' parents.

From time to time I see other teachers who have apparently forgotten which party is the adult. Teenage teachers and assistants often fall into one of two extremes—emphasizing their authority in nitpicking ways or enjoying being one of the children and getting to play. Some ineffective methods of discipline just correct themselves with maturity and experience, but with a society emphasizing children's "rights" and de-emphasizing adults' authority and responsibility toward children, it seems good to consider what it means to be the adult in the classroom.

When inexperienced teachers come into a classroom, often the first thing they see is how cute the children are. But some children resent being considered cute. Others take advantage of it and manipulate the unsuspecting teacher. I had a ten-year-old student who managed two or three times to find her way into the lap of a student teacher, where she braided the college student's hair instead of listening to the lesson. The scenario was quite distracting to the other boys and girls, regardless of the warm memories it may have given the college student, and I firmly stopped it.

One day at summer camp the devotion for the day was well suited for an outside location. I told the junior girls we were going outside, and immediately several started whining. "Oh, can't we stay inside, please? We don't want to go outside." When I told them again we were going outside, a few pouted.

We went outside, but I had lost the devotional spirit of the group. The issue bothered me as an example of how adult authority has been eroded since I was a child (not that long ago). Clearly the girls saw the issue as a democratic one: Let's vote and see what most of the girls want. I saw it as a relatively unimportant decision: It's better to go outside, the teacher says we're going outside, so there is no need for an argument or further discussion.

In a similar setting, I could choose differently. If, for example, I had merely thought that the girls would love being outside on such a beautiful day, I could have changed my mind and stayed inside at their request. What would not have been appropriate—but what I have seen inexperienced teachers do many times—is something like this:

Teacher: I've decided it might be nice to have devotions outside today. What do you think?

Girl: No, it's too hot. Let's stay in the cabin.

Two other girls: Yeah, let's stay here.

Teacher: Come on, please—it's really not that hot. It'll be nice. Don't you want to go outside?

Four or five girls: No.

Teacher: OK, we'll stay here.

(Alternately, Teacher, suddenly making up her mind: We're going outside, and that's final.)

That scene looks as if the teacher is just one of the girls giving a suggestion and trying to talk the other girls into following her. It is appropriate sometimes for the teacher to change his or her mind because the class has an alternate idea that works, and it's not appropriate for the teacher to bully the class and let them think they can't even suggest alternatives. But the teacher needs to be the leader and the one ultimately responsible for the decision, whatever it is.

Here's another scenario (OK, I admit it, I've been there):

Teacher: Class, let's go . . .

Billy (seeing something else that looks attractive, interrupts): Oh, cool—let's go over there. (Half the class follows him.)

Teacher (with a shrug, to the rest of the class): Yes, let's go do whatever Billy is doing.

By the way, part of being an adult is getting past the need to prove you're an adult by knowing when to be something other than "the one in charge." For instance, when a boy in about third grade trips and falls down, he may stay on the ground with his eyes closed until someone notices him—apparently his way of turning a clumsy accident into something he did for a joke. The teacher can say, "David, get up right now!" or she can say, "Hey, David's dead. Looks like we need to bury him." Not only does the second response get better results—usually the child jumps up instantly to prove he's alive—but it shows that you have a sense of humor.

One small key to effective discipline may be insisting that children address you using a title, not just your first name. "Miss Sandra" or "Mrs. Chambers" or "Uncle Stan" reinforces subtly that you are not on the same level as the child.

The teacher's first responsibility in a classroom is not to be the children's friend. Ideally, their love and respect will come as the teacher loves and respects the students. But boys and girls need authority, guidance, and protection, and only a firm but fair adult can provide those. The smart teacher expects obedience (and not just eventually), attention, response from students, learning, and application of that learning.

For Thought

1. What do you believe is the proper balance between allowing student input and insisting on your plan? Do you maintain that balance?

2. In what areas might your lack of maturity hurt your teaching? In contrast, in what areas might your sense of your own maturity make it hard for children to get close to you?

22

WANTED: CHRISTIAN MEN IN THE CLASSROOM

But as for you, speak the things which are proper for sound doctrine: that the older men be sober, reverent, temperate, sound in faith, in love, in patience; . . . Likewise exhort the young men to be sober-minded, in all things showing yourself to be a pattern of good works; in doctrine showing integrity, reverence, incorruptibility, sound speech that cannot be condemned . . . Speak these things, exhort, and rebuke with all authority. Let no one despise you.

(TITUS 2:1–2, 6–8, 15)

For several years after I began teaching in my church's club program, I prayed for men to see the need to become involved with our children. Today we have several male teachers. All too often, though, teaching children is seen as "women's work."

The need for men's involvement in the classroom is urgent. Many children grow up knowing few positive male role models in their early years. The problem is extreme for boys from single-parent homes who see older boys selling drugs or involved in gangs. But girls also need male role models. Little girls may not have a daddy at home, or they may not see him much. Children who deal with an angry or abusive father may find that a loving male teacher helps them to understand how God can be a good Father. Men who love children have a chance for great influence in their lives.

Women, of course, bring strengths of their own to working with boys and girls. Many women have a more intuitive sense when dealing with children, combined with more experience and less awkwardness. Plus, historically, working with children has often been seen as somehow unmanly.

That many women are good with children is readily accepted; I'd like to focus here on what men bring to a children's program, so that whether you are a man or a woman you can do your part to let men use their strengths in your class. If you are a woman, be aware that many men expect women to be the experts when it comes to children, and unfortunately that means they may hang back and let you take the lead in discipline. As we'll explore here, that is counterproductive.

Men have a possibility for authority that women can only envy; usually men's voices can convey "I mean it" more convincingly. And children who have begun to test authority are well served by having an adult who can accept their challenges, remain firm, and still like them. Boys, especially, seem to believe a man's "final word" more than they believe the same ultimatum from a woman. So all teachers benefit when the program includes a man who is known for being fair but also known for being someone nobody can sneak past.

I think of it this way: When a fifth- or sixth-grade boy is beginning to figure out what it means to be a man, he may bluster and argue and charge like a bull against anyone who blocks his path. He needs someone who is strong enough to stand in his way without moving and thus earn his respect.

I can speak as firmly as I like, but if a boy weighs as much as I do, at some point he is likely to ponder just how tough I am. That is particularly true if he decides it would be wimpy to obey a woman. When I'm dealing with such a boy, I welcome a man who will come alongside and reinforce what kind of behavior is expected, supporting my authority and not undermining it. That's good for the boy and for me. Once my authority has been backed up, usually the boy is more likely to listen the next time.

For the most part, I have found that I'm quite effective with boys because I respond to children matter-of-factly. Boys past the age of four or five are very sensitive to being considered cute, and some boys put their defenses up against women. My response to them allows them to lower those defenses. But any woman's effectiveness with boys is limited, particularly once they pass the first few years of grade school. And if she is regularly forced to be tough and be the final authority with hard cases, she may lose some chances to be the softer kind of teacher that children need in a woman.

Through the years I have had to deal with a lot of boys' fights when a man was unavailable or unwilling to get involved. A man's physical presence, his more commanding voice, and his awareness of what it is like to be a boy puts him in a better position in such instances. Boys who are fighting and trying to prove their manhood are well served by a man who comes along and separates them but who at the same time also shows to them what it really means to be a man.

Unfortunately, many churches have a harder time recruiting men than women—or even seeing the need to recruit men. Yet Christ took time to bless the children who came to Him, and He even rebuked His disciples when they tried to keep the little ones away. He spoke of the importance of a child's faith. He spoke blessings on those who treat children well and curses on those who endanger their faith. Men and women are both needed in this crucial work.

For Thought

1. If you are a woman: How many men are involved in your teaching situation? What strengths do they bring? How can they be even more effective? If your program does not have enough men, have you prayed about this need?

2. If you are a man: In what ways have you taken advantage of the uniquely male strengths enumerated in this chapter? How can you support other teachers without appearing to be taking over because they are ineffective? What are two things the boys in your class need from you? What are two things the girls need?

23

MOVING INTO YOUR STUDENTS' WORLD

So, affectionately longing for you, we were
well pleased to impart to you not only the
gospel of God, but also our own lives,
because you had become dear to us.

(1 THESSALONIANS 2:8)

Four years ago, I decided to enter the world of the kids I teach—literally. A friend and I moved into a child-saturated neighborhood one block east of our church. We are deliberately child-friendly. In the summer the freezer always holds treats, given free to any child who asks. A few children come into the house (with parental permission and with the safeguard of always having at least two children at a time). Although I am single and have no children of my own, the bottom shelf of my bookcase is lined with children's books for these visitors. I stay stocked up on craft materials and coloring books. Sometimes I make cookies with the kids who come over. Sometimes they put makeup on my roommate or dance with her around the living room until the landlady comes downstairs to complain about the noise.

I think of my time with the children as being something far more meaningful than playtime. It's immersing them in love shown by focused attention. It's training them in social skills and Christian attitudes. It's teaching them reading skills and creativity. It's keeping them safe. It's being available to answer questions. And, as much as any of these things, it's having an opportunity to observe them in their world during their unguarded interactions with each other.

Some interesting dynamics have evolved. When I come home from work, sometimes children I don't know call me by name. Originally our neighbors called us "the church ladies" because they saw us walking to church with our Bibles. Now the children know us as the people with freezer pops. I think the combination is a pretty good one: the church ladies who give out freezer pops. And I don't know whether or not there's a connection, but a few more of the neighborhood children have come to our church since we moved in.

Getting involved in children's lives doesn't have to mean moving to a new home, but it is crucial to connect with children beyond Sunday morning. Here are some ideas for such connections: Children love to get mail, so send each member of your class a picture post-card or even a small "care package." Partner with another teacher and make short visits to the children's homes. Such visits can be quite natural at Christmas, the week the child has a birthday, or around some other special occasion.

One day I stopped by the house of two children I knew; one was in my class that year, and one had been the previous year. The younger student, Joshua, had never paid much attention to me in class. But as I knocked at his door, he rode up on a bicycle accompanied by a friend. Even in front of his friend, Joshua's wide grin and enthusiastic greeting showed clear delight at having me visit him.

During the church service when members greet each other, make a point of greeting each child within a few rows of you. If you see that the class below yours has a disruptive child in it, learn that child's name and greet him in a friendly way each week. Once he reaches your class, he may already think of you as a friend and not just a disciplinarian. Noted pastor Charles Spurgeon said long ago, "The fault of many teachers is that they do not get their children near them; but endeavour to foster in their scholars a kind of awful respect. Before you can teach children, you must get the silver key of kindness to unlock their hearts, and so secure their attention."

Take groups of kids to the park, the zoo, or the mall. If you have children of your own, include some of your students in a family outing. Have your class over for a party. And during the class hour, look for opportunities to connect with individual children.

Billy, one of my fourth graders, was going through a defiant stage. Neither his parents nor I could quite figure out how to rein him in. So each week I looked for him after the Sunday morning service just to say hello. In that setting, I could be sure to have a nondisciplinary encounter, and I was quietly saying, "I like you. I'm not going to ignore you and just speak to the adults." One week as I left church, a child's voice yelled, "Bye, Cheryl." I turned to see Billy, half a parking lot away, getting into the car with his parents. I smiled, waved, and whispered, "God, thank You." It was not an instant fix, but in later encounters with Billy I had a foundation of mutual respect earned by the hard work of deliberate encounters outside of class.

For Thought

1. Would your students describe you as someone who really likes children? Before class, do you cluster with other teachers or interact with boys and girls?

2. Which children in your class have been resisting your efforts to teach them? What are two practical ways you can interact with them outside of class?

24

UNDERSTANDING ACROSS CULTURAL LINES

I have become all things to all men, that I might by all means save some.

(1 CORINTHIANS 9:22)

There is neither Jew nor Greek, there is neither slave nor free, there is neither male nor female; for you are all one in Christ Jesus.

(GALATIANS 3:28)

I remember the first time I taught black children. I was a freshman in Bible college and had several years of experience teaching kids, yet I was unprepared for cross-cultural teaching and found the year frustrating. Songs that white children in Phoenix loved to sing brought less than enthusiastic singing from black children in inner-city Chicago. I had developed a teaching style that included walking back and forth across the front of the classroom and putting body language into a story while I told it, but now when I stood while teaching, this particular class seemed to lose interest. To keep their attention, I had to stay seated.

More than ten years have gone by since then. I have attended a mixed-race church on the border of Chicago for the last decade. Much of that time I have taught the church's children, most of them black. I rent a house in an all-black neighborhood one block from church. Many of the church's boys and girls live within two or three blocks of me, and many have seemed more open to me since I deliberately became a part of their world. Today I'm slightly more comfortable working with black children—with their extra level of exuberance and loyalty to friends and family—than I am with white kids. Over the last several years, I have learned a lot of small lessons about cross-cultural ministry to children. Although my experience is largely limited to white or black boys and girls, I believe much of what I have learned could apply in any cross-cultural setting.

I have learned sensitivity and teachability. I have spent a lot of hours reading black literature and attempting to understand African-American history. A person ministering in a Hispanic area would be well-served by learning some Spanish. It's inappropriate to come in with the attitude of an expert arriving to fix a troubled community. Inner-city communities often see eager young people coming in to "save" the community, then leaving in discouragement in a year or eighteen months. Minority residents, therefore, may show less enthusiasm than the novice somehow assumes he has earned just by showing up. I was fortunate in that I didn't have to earn acceptance in my neighborhood, because my neighbors already trusted my church's reputation. I have become a member of the community— which is, incidentally, the friendliest neighborhood I have ever lived in. At block parties, I'm a neighbor, not a white person.

I have learned to notice what attitudes and words from white people build roadblocks. For example, in days of slavery, grown men were called "boy" by their masters. That is still a point of sensitivity for some African-Americans. Teachers who say, "Get over here, boy," to a misbehaving student don't mean to offend, but they may do so. I've also heard white people casually make comments such as "All right, you've got yourself a slave!" when they see that a friend has a young person (black or white) cleaning the house for the day. But such thoughtless joking can really damage trust.

As I've come "inside," I've seen another angle to familiar images of minority communities. For instance, many preschool children in my neighborhood know more about sex than I did when I was twelve. I've seen four-year-olds doing sophisticated sexual dances as they play in the sprinkler and have watched six-year-olds sing along to vile songs spewing from a passerby's boom box. It helps me understand why a ten-year-old could tell me, "Everyone's always saying, 'Wait until marriage to have sex,' but that's not possible." A deeper understanding has helped me learn not to avoid the issue in class (it's a safe bet that all my third graders know about sex already), not to be too easily shocked, and not to consider myself morally superior because sexual purity is less of a struggle for me than for my minority students.

The stereotypes of minority communities, true and false, are well known. In my experience, black people do not readily admit to problems in their community in front of white people they don't know well. That's likely because it seems virtually all most white people know of minority communities are the "problems."

I have found a large number of positive cultural traits in the black community, traits of which I was only vaguely aware before moving into it. I call those "positive stereotypes." The most significant of those, in a functioning community such as the one where I live, is community strength. Neighbors collect money for a grieving family that has lost a child or suffered from a fire. Hospitality is important. I have found mothers looking out for each others' kids, older kids looking out for younger (younger siblings and cousins are treated more like friends than pests), an awareness of community needs, friendliness even to strangers who come through. Children well know their grandparents, aunts, uncles, and cousins. In minority neighborhoods, children are "our" children, cared for or gently reprimanded by anyone in the neighborhood.

The church is a significant part of community life. I have seen neighbors attend a prayer vigil held in front of an apartment unit that had just experienced a mind-boggling crisis. I have seen neighbors risk stepping between young men who were fighting. Politicians go door-to-door here, because the direct touch is still meaningful.

Many of the boys and girls I know read several years below their grade level. Yet their verbal skills tend to be good, because they interact with friends of various ages and because they live in an oral culture. At camp, where some white children come from white-dominant areas, white children often seem to see louder, more verbal black children as aggressive and are intimidated by them. Yet the difference is merely cultural. Part of my role in such settings is to understand the reactions of both sides, to try to keep them from the natural tendency to pull away from each other and then talk about each other in their own clusters, and to help them trust each other.

For Further Study

1. Do you have children of a different culture in your class or in your church? What are two ways you can better understand the way they see life?

2. Ask someone from a different culture, or someone who works with people from a different culture, to recommend two or three books that will help you better understand that culture.

25

ENCOURAGING THE IRREGULAR ATTENDEE

But Jesus called them to Him and said, "Let the little children come to Me, and do not forbid them; for of such is the kingdom of God."

(LUKE 18:16)

When I started teaching my first Sunday school class, Gina had been filling out the attendance chart. I let her continue doing so, because I didn't care who did it as long as it got done. One morning, she asked me, "Can I fill out the enrollment?"

"You may this week, anyway," I said. Then Krissy arrived and asked to fill out the chart. Krissy's father dropped her off occasionally, and he picked her up when Sunday school was over. She had come only two or three times in the five months I had been teaching. Casually, I told her, "I already told Gina she could, but if you are here next week you may do it then."

I didn't know the importance of filling out that attendance chart. The following week, Krissy was the first one there. She asked me eagerly, "Can I fill out the enrollment?"

"Sure," I told her, "I said you could."

Irregular attendees are part of every class. Most of them are brought by neighbors or baby-sitters, or their parents drop them off whenever the children ask to go. Sometimes they walk from nearby homes. Some irregular attendees have Christian parents who can't decide what church to attend or who usually attend the church service but not Sunday school. Some come from homes of unbelievers who have a vague sense that their children should be in church whether the parents are or not, or where the children themselves feel the urge to attend. In many cases, it is the child who decides whether or not to come. You can gauge the interest of such a child by the frequency of his attendance.

Don't overlook the importance of ministering to such children, even if they are challenging students or they seldom come. One of the most moving books I have read in recent years is *Glenda's Story*, a book about a little girl who was unloved throughout childhood. Writing her story as an adult, Glenda Revell says that in childhood she often walked by a nearby church and "longed to go inside. I thought God lived there and would be more likely to answer my prayers if I prayed in church."[1] She soon found out that a girl from her school attended the church, so she timidly asked her mother for permission to go. Glenda reports,

> Surprisingly, she said yes. How thankful I am for her consent, for the years I spent in that church were a wonderful comfort to me.
>
> On Sunday mornings, rain or shine, I dressed myself and walked to church. Sometimes I was the first to arrive. When that happened, I just plopped myself down on the front steps and waited, full of joy and anticipation.
>
> I wonder how I must have looked to those people. Was my hair brushed? Was I clean? What did they think of the little girl who came to Sunday school alone and sat, solitary, on the front row during the church service? Did anyone even notice? Did anyone care? I don't know the answer to any of those questions, but this I do know: I, who was particularly sensitive to the attitudes and opinions of others, never felt rejected or unwanted there. It was a marvelous place for me to grow and thrive.[2]

Glenda did not accept Jesus as her Savior until years later, but during the years of her childhood, beginning the year she started school, she made the trek to church each week to meet God. Do you have such children in your church? Do you have one or two in your class?

It is especially important that you attempt to form a personal relationship with the irregular attendee. Ask for his phone number, and call him during the week. Greet him by name when he comes into the room. Ask him questions and listen carefully to his answers. Let him be involved in the class; let him feel your class is a place he belongs.

For several months last year, a small group of children sat together in my church without an adult. The children were very young: kindergarten, first grade, and second grade. When I saw them before the service, I often sat with them. If I did not see them, usually they sat alone. Whether I joined them or they were by themselves, I noticed that they sat quietly and attentively. I asked about the children and heard that they were in foster care. Somehow their hearts, like Glenda's, were drawn to church.

Our church has other children who come unaccompanied by adults. Fortunately, we have usually been good at "adopting" these children. Some church family has a child sit with them and may even contact the child during the week. Occasionally, parents of these children come, thank us profusely, and promise to come to the church that loves their children. However, the parents rarely start coming. To some churches, that would represent failure. Yet I think the God who pulled children into His lap would not see it that way.

Notes

1. Glenda Revell, *Glenda's Story: Led by Grace* (Lincoln, Neb.: Gateway to Joy, 1994), 46.
2. Ibid., 47.

For Thought

1. Do you know the family connections of all the children in your class, including the irregular attendees? If not, is there someone in your church who could help you discover that information?

2. Does your church contain any children who bring themselves to church? If you don't know, ask somebody. As you see such children in church, make a point of greeting them warmly.

26

DEALING WITH DISINTERESTED KIDS

O God, You have taught me from my youth; and
to this day I declare Your wondrous works.

(PSALM 71:17)

Ben kept it no secret that he didn't particularly like me. He avoided making eye contact, and sometimes he sighed or rolled his eyes when I looked at him. Efforts to get to know him proved futile because of his resistance. Since Ben was also less mature than the other children in my class, my solution was easy: I asked that he be moved to a class of younger children that overlapped with his grade, hoping he'd find a better fit in it.

But usually solutions to disinterested children aren't quite that obvious. If many members of the class seem disinterested, the teacher and students are often all frustrated. Even if it's only one or two students who don't respond to the teacher, not only are those students possibly not learning much, but they can manage to distract the rest of the class. The problem can't really be ignored, even though solutions are often difficult.

A child might be disinterested in his class for any of several reasons: boredom, discomfort with the teacher or other children, inability to understand the lesson, a sense (true or false) that the teacher doesn't like him, family problems, hostility or lack of interest toward Christian things, learning disabilities, or some other issue. Sometimes bored kids are the ones who have been in church all their lives and who know all the "Sunday school stories" by heart.

A basic element of keeping class interest is being sure kids are actually learning. It may be time to challenge them a bit more than you have been doing. But sometimes the problem is at the other end of the spectrum: They don't understand what the teacher is saying because her teaching is too complex for them.

Good teaching encourages good listening (though it doesn't guarantee it). The teacher who knows her class and who interacts with her students personally in and out of the classroom will have better attention from them. The teacher who works on her storytelling ability and develops other skills, including the ability to keep a class moving by organizing the class period and supplies ahead of time, will hold class interest more effectively. And the teacher who prays for her students by name during the week will discover that she has a better spiritual connection with them and cares about them more, both of which aid in effective teaching.

Involving children helps them feel less like spectators and more like a part of the class. It undercuts boredom, allows them to move, and helps them focus more for better learning. Much teaching can take place by means of singing and learning memory verses. Some children really enjoy Bible review games. No method should be used *just* because children like it—many minutes are wasted in thousands of classes singing meaningless songs such as "Father Abraham"—but methods that fit your teaching purpose and involve children serve a dual purpose.

If you have a disinterested child who likes maps, show the class on a map where the lesson took place. You may even be able to enlist the child's help ahead of time and let *him* show the map to the class. Using visual aids, adjusting your volume or speed of talking, and involving the children by asking them questions can all help keep them focused.

During one summer program, the teacher spent so much time on preliminary games and other activities that she had barely started the lesson five minutes after she was due to dismiss the class to swim time. Fifteen minutes later, she was still talking, my girls were squirming, and one child was whispering, "What time is it?" It's easy to argue that a Bible lesson is more important than swim time, but keeping distracted children twenty minutes extra lends itself to resentment of Bible teaching, not to learning.

Sometimes teachers continue teaching exactly as planned after they have lost the attention of their entire class. They plow through the lesson in lecture mode, apparently oblivious to class response. Perhaps they hope at least one kid somehow learns something. Doing whatever is necessary to get through may mean angrily shushing noisy students, or it may mean just ignoring the noise and speeding through. But children in such a class soon compare Bible teaching with their least favorite subject in school: something to endure.

When you lose class attention, it is far better to slow down and refocus the lesson. Interact with the class by asking questions. Have them supply a sound effect or repeat something a character said, or have them look at the passage in their Bibles and then ask them a question about it. Such flexibility can not only get a class back on track; it also helps you know what they are thinking and lets them see that you care whether or not they learn.

One day I was teaching the very familiar story of Noah and the ark, and I lost the attention of a few students. I paused for a moment so the kids would look at me to see what I was going to do. Since the lesson was at the point where Noah and his family and the animals were in the boat and the rain was coming down, I had the children do the "rain forest" camp activity. First, all the kids rub their hands together, then they slap their hands on their knees, then they stamp their feet, following the teacher's lead for each. If done correctly, it's easy to imagine the noise of a thunderstorm outside. I quieted them by going back to the hand rubbing—and had their attention for the rest of the lesson.

For Action

1. Do you ever face the problem of disinterest in your class? Is the problem with one or two students or a bigger portion of the class? What do you think is the biggest handicap to their interest?

2. What are two things you can do next week to rope in the disinterested children? Include your ideas in your lesson plan.

27

INTERACTING WITH THE CHILD WHO REALLY NEEDS YOU

[Jesus] said to them, "Whoever receives this little child in My name receives Me; and whoever receives Me receives Him who sent Me. For he who is least among you all will be great."

(LUKE 9:48)

I have known one young friend, who is now in high school, for several years. I first remember her as a child whose parents had recently fled danger in Liberia. She often shyly held out a book and asked me to read it, or she read it to me. Later I was her counselor at camp, and later still I was the adult greeting a teenage girl with a hug. Although she has a family who loves her, I am an adult friend who knew her and loved her in a time of adjustment to a new culture.

I had only sporadic interaction with junior high students until last year, when a large number of kids I'd taught in earlier years graduated into junior high. But I have had two or three individual relationships with junior high students based on this principle: *If a child seeks me out, I will consider a relationship with that child to be an opportunity and a responsibility from God.* I take such love as an honor and give my own in return.

Several years ago, a fourth-grade girl in my class reminded me of myself at her age. Charlotte was uncomfortable among her peers, so she gravitated to adults instead. I gave her the attention she seemed to relish, but I also looked for creative opportunities to help her make friends among her classmates.

When kids were asked to choose partners for a game, Charlotte instantly pulled out of the group. She said she wanted to see what they were playing before she decided whether she wanted to play. Her action was self-defeating. All the other girls chose partners, and she was left out. Later, she separated from the other students again by sitting at a table by herself during project time. I made her sit at the table with the others and gave her an "assignment": to compliment at least one other girl on her project. I was teaching her basic social skills, and she proudly did my small assignments to please me.

When such a relationship has been established, often it continues after I no longer teach the child. I'm not in a position to formally teach her anymore, but my life and my love make her open to my words—perhaps even more open than she was in a classroom setting. Our conversations may not be about anything important most of the time, but these children readily bring their needs and their questions about God.

Many teachers avoid having special relationships with individual students, thinking of that as favoritism. It's true that other children will quickly resent special favors shown to one child *within the class hour.* If the child becomes known as "teacher's pet," he may become even more isolated from his peers. But the reality is that only a few children in any particular class will seek out the teacher for such attention. And if one child regularly stays after class to talk with you or seeks you out after the church service, she is making a request for your attention that the other kids aren't making, and it is appropriate for you to respond to that request and give her extra attention outside of class.

Most children will have their primary needs for adult relationships met elsewhere, especially if they have good relationships with their parents. You can't fulfill the role of mentor/adult friend with every one of your students, so focus on the children who seem to click with you.

Children seek such attention for numerous reasons:

- Something about you appeals to this particular child; she has chosen you for some of the same reasons you might choose a friend or a hero.
- The child receives little adult attention, so she needs attention from you.
- The child is more comfortable with adults than with children, so she'd rather hang out with the teacher than with the other students.
- Her world is unstable, perhaps due to parental divorce or some other factor that feels out of control, and she needs someone bigger than she is to help her feel secure.

An adult's acceptance seems to be more basic to a child's sense of well-being than peer friendships. Without an adult who deeply loves him, he will lack confidence, and he will lack the skills needed for social interaction.

What does a child who seeks your attention need from you? He needs your time and attention and the sense you *like* him. He needs you to listen to him. In many cases, the child also needs something else, such as help with reading or social skills. An adult who has earned the trust of a child may occasionally be in a position to learn of deeper needs and struggles.

It is necessary to respect parents' rules and to talk respectfully of them to their children, even if a child comes to you for sympathy. That does not always mean defending parents, but it means listening without jumping in with reasons of your own that the parents aren't very nice. It may mean gently pointing out areas where the child's actions or words have been disrespectful. Your role is to support parents and help them teach their kids, not to undermine their authority. Obviously that doesn't mean overlooking clear evidence of abuse—you should discuss that with your pastor—but usually a child just needs someone who listens and loves him and shows him Christ.

Often it's necessary to earn the trust of a child's parents. If Mom and Dad seem uneasy when you call the house, don't call. Show interest when the child seeks you out and greet him in a public place, such as church. But if you pursue the relationship beyond the parents' comfort level, they may intervene and cut off contact entirely, and that may hurt your ministry in other ways.

For Thought

1. Has a particular child in your class or outside it sought you out for a relationship? What has been your response?

2. What aspects of your background, training, experience, or personality might lend you credibility or skill in dealing with particular children? Can you think of children who fit one of those categories?

PART 4

THE PURPOSE OF TEACHING

How are our children being formed? Do they know themselves primarily as citizens of the kingdom of God? Do we and our offspring look, act, talk, and think like people who are shaped by the narratives of our faith, by God's Revelation?

—MARVA J. DAWN,
Is It a Lost Cause? Having the Heart of God for the Church's Children (Grand Rapids: Eerdmans, 1997), 3.

Our churches might not be the most "successful" ones in town if we nurture children for the rigors of discipleship instead of catering to their consumerist tastes. Are we willing to wage war against the principle of Mammon for the sake of genuine spiritual growth in our children and ourselves? . . . I believe that if Christian churches truly manifested the gracious emptying and self-giving of Jesus, that love would draw their children into the community.

—MARVA DAWN, *Is It a Lost Cause?* 149.

28

SUGARCOATING SCRIPTURE

Behold, I long for Your precepts; revive me in Your
righteousness. . . . Let Your tender mercies come to me,
that I may live; for Your law is my delight. . . . Oh, how
I love Your law! It is my meditation all the day. . . .
How sweet are Your words to my taste, sweeter than
honey to my mouth!

(PSALM 119:40, 77, 97, 103)

A familiar maxim says that a spoonful of sugar helps the medicine go down. The problem is that America has translated the "spoonful of sugar" into a philosophy of life for all ages. We no longer believe it's acceptable for work to be dull, for child-rearing to be a sacrifice, for education to be laborious . . . or for worship to be hard work.

In *Amusing Ourselves to Death,* Neil Postman says, "Television's principal contribution to educational philosophy is the idea that teaching and entertainment are inseparable."[1] What is true of the public school classroom is now also true of the Christian classroom— we assume that learning has to be fun.

But nowhere in Scripture are we guaranteed that coming to God will always be delightful. In fact, those meeting up with God quite often fell on their faces in terror or reverent awe. The Bible certainly never indicates that Christianity will always be *fun* or that its primary purpose is our entertainment. The Old Testament tells of several occasions when the whole community, including older children, gathered to listen to the law of God read for hours at a time (Deuteronomy 31:10–13; Nehemiah 8:2–3). Jesus fed the five thousand only after they had listened to Him for so many hours He worried they'd faint with hunger on their way home. Then He chastised the people who came running the next time they saw Him because they expected another free, miraculous lunch.

When we merely ask, "Do my students like Sunday school?" the answer can be a quick yes. But that's not the primary question. We should be asking, "Are the children I teach learning to love God and the Bible, learning more about Him, and becoming adequately prepared for their eventual role as adult worshipers?" Have we been successful if children like coming to a church's programs even if they learn virtually nothing? I think not.

I'm not saying that Christian education shouldn't be interesting. But gauging its success by how *fun* it is—by how much children like it—is like judging an army officer's success by the glowing reports his soldiers write back home.

The criterion of "fun" gets its cues from the wrong place—from culture rather than Scripture. It also trains people in the wrong habits. Children and even adults often approach Scripture with the same lighthearted spirit they use for games or other trivial tasks. If we try too hard to make children *like* Sunday school, we may find that, when adults, they will come to church only if the service contains the delights of a juvenile Sunday school class.

We add a spoonful of sugar to medicine only if it tastes bad. Burying Scripture too deeply in a sea of fun activities may suggest that Scripture itself is quite unpleasant.

So, should we sit children down and lecture them on the intricacies of Paul's theology? Of course not. It's no solution to turn the beauty of Scripture into a speech that boys and girls can neither understand nor enjoy. On the other hand, if by the time our students reach adulthood they still can't handle deep teaching, something is clearly wrong. (See Hebrews 5:12–13.) Somehow our teaching needs to lay the groundwork for the future.

Recently in my class of second and third graders, I gave an assignment that most Christian education experts would probably consider better suited for junior or junior high students. I got out a map. Then I gave each child an index card on which I'd written a Scripture reference and three questions: "Where did Paul go? Who went with him? What did they do?" Not only did the children enjoy the challenge, but they were able to see that they could read and understand parts of the Bible. (See appendix A for more details on this assignment and some other Bible studies.)

Children need to see the Word of God raw sometimes. They need to handle the Bible, turn its pages, fall in love with its words and its truths. Most of it may be beyond their reach without adult help, but some of it is not. Give them those understandable parts as often as you can—uncooked, undiluted. Develop their taste for the Word of God by allowing them to sample it for themselves.

And when a passage must be predigested by you before they can chew it, remember that your job is still to teach the Word, not to entertain. Such teaching is less popular with Christian education experts and with many parents. It is easier to ensure that kids enjoy Sunday school than to teach in such a way that they love Scripture and the God who has given it. But dare we settle for less than the second?

The Bible is a profound, mysterious, life-changing book. It is the power of God unto salvation (Romans 1:16). It is great treasure, a strong light, and everlasting truth. Let it be exciting, but don't coat it with so many sugary substances that children in your class become accustomed to the sweet coatings and are intimidated by the Book itself. Good teaching will help your boys and girls grow to adulthood knowing the Book and loving its Author. Rather than the spoonful of sweetener given with medicine, perhaps good teaching is more like a sprinkling of sugar over strawberries.

Note

1. Neil Postman, *Amusing Ourselves to Death: Public Discourse in the Age of Show Business* (New York: Penguin, 1985), 146.

For Thought

1. What aspects of your teaching obscure or sugarcoat the Word of God rather than illuminating it? Do you sometimes use fun activities that have virtually nothing to do with the lesson or visuals that distract from the point being made?

2. When might you be guilty of the other extreme—presenting Scripture in such a way that it looks boring? For example, when do you find yourself lapsing into lecture mode?

29

THE PURPOSE OF CHRISTIAN EDUCATION

And my speech and my preaching were not
with persuasive words of human wisdom, but
in demonstration of the Spirit and of power,
that your faith should not be in the wisdom of
men but in the power of God.

(1 CORINTHIANS 2:4–5)

A few years ago I heard a twenty-year veteran of teaching Sunday school say it was essential for Christian teachers to use the most up-to-date visual technology possible. He emphasized that children are used to high-quality videos, therefore we need to use them as often as we can. But such thinking merely restates "keeping up with the Joneses" for Sunday school. I believe that by asking the wrong question, "What do secular experts use with children?" he discovered the wrong answer.

I changed around the question to ask, "What are today's children *not* getting?"

For one thing, most children today aren't getting much nondisciplinary eye contact with adults or one-on-one attention from them, partly because of TV and video.

Most boys and girls also aren't growing up hearing good storytelling. Yet youngsters learn much about their world through stories. A child learns to admire the good by loving admirable people, whether Moses or George Washington. A well-told story, told by a live human being, true to Scripture, has much more power than a well-produced video. A lesson taught by an attentive, experienced, imaginative teacher can be personalized in a way a video never can.

And, most important, most children aren't being taught much about the Bible or spiritual or moral principles. This was brought home to me in force during a vacation Bible school at my church. When I asked what Christians can do to obey Jesus, the only answers twenty children could think of were "Don't steal" and "Be nice." When I asked what the Bible says about obeying parents, none of them had an answer.

A few months later, in a Sunday school class of second and third graders, I mentioned Shadrach, Meshach, and Abednego. One child asked in surprise, "Did that really happen?" I assured him the story was true. I was caught off guard by his next question: "They really made those chocolate Easter bunnies?" This child from a church family knew nothing about a familiar Bible story except what a children's video had done with it.

How can boys and girls who are nurtured on TV, video games, the Internet, and movies at home, in the classroom, and even in church ever value the role that suffering plays in the Christian life? How can they be prepared for missionary service, for persecution, even for martyrdom? There is joy in the Christian life *within* difficult times, but pampered Christians are unlikely to find it. American believers as a whole are soft, out-of-shape Christians who know almost nothing of being countercultural believers able to "turn the world upside down" (see Acts 17:6).

We are made for God's glory, not our own comfort or pleasure. Somehow we must re-capture the sense that God's glory is of greater urgency than our fun. Somehow we must desire God's glory more than we want our own prayers answered. And somehow we must communicate a greater vision of God to our children. As Marva Dawn pointed out, "The only thing the Church does that no one else can do is worship the triune God."[1]

In spite of our choosing to emphasize "fun" teaching methods, church children still talk about video games with much greater enthusiasm than about the Bible—and they certainly *know* more about the games than about Scripture. Boys and girls today are easily bored and want a constant change of scene. If we try to compete on the same level as the rest of their world, not only are we failing to train them for biblical Christianity, but when we compete with culture, we lose. Mark DeVries writes,

> I don't know of any youth ministry that can, week in and week out, compete with a 92-million dollar movie. Compared to most other options young people have for entertainment, we don't have a chance. If we train our youth to expect entertainment from church, we can be assured that when things get a little slow, they will be switching the channel to somebody else's show. . . . We are in danger of teaching them that the Christian life will always be a party. Some Christian sociologists have called this generation of Christian youth "God's little brats." They are growing up with the expectation that they should never be bored, never be uncomfortable, never have to do without.[2]

When we put Christianity in the same category as the latest movie, last month's lesson can be ignored as readily as last month's video game or movie can be forgotten. Special ef-fects should never replace or cancel out quality teaching. After all, even for boys and girls, "faith comes by hearing"—not by seeing or by experiencing—"and hearing by the Word of God."

What can a teacher accomplish in one hour Sunday morning if he or she attempts to meet children's true needs rather than focusing on whatever they find most fun? When I explored that question, I realized that four primary focuses are essential to good teaching. Four things work together to give our children "hope and a future." The teacher must:

- Know the children and their world
- Introduce them to a God who is big enough for their worship and awe
- Show them how they can know God directly
- Be a bridge connecting them to the larger body of Christ, the church

Success in teaching can never be measured in numbers or in excitement, but it can be judged by how well your teaching measures up against these harder-to-measure goals, which are the focus of this book.

Notes

1. Marva Dawn, *Is It a Lost Cause? Having the Heart of God for the Church's Children* (Grand Rapids: Eerdmans, 1997), 65.
2. Mark DeVries, *Family-Based Youth Ministry* (Downers Grove, Ill.: InterVarsity, 1994), 153.

For Evaluation

1. Write a one-sentence definition, in your own words, of the purpose of Christian education.

2. How well does your own teaching match up to what you believe teaching should be?

30

WHY DO YOU TEACH?

*Finally, my brethren, be strong in the Lord
and in the power of His might.*

(EPHESIANS 6:10)

*Let us hold fast the confession of our hope
without wavering, for He who promised is
faithful.*

(HEBREWS 10:23)

A few years ago I threw my own private pity party because nobody was noticing me.
The climax came when I was walking toward home with a friend and one of my students came running toward us. The student, Latrice, opened her arms for a hug, so I opened mine—and Latrice hugged my friend, who had been her counselor at camp the week before. In her excitement over seeing her counselor, she didn't even notice *me*, her *teacher*.

My feeling of jealousy caught me off guard. Is that really why I teach—to be noticed and applauded by my children? Motives like that will be burned up in the judgment. And a motive like that is bound to lead to disappointment here on earth. Most of the time, children take love for granted. Their capacity for affection is great, but they aren't good at noticing when adults are having a bad day. They aren't good at making sure adult feelings aren't hurt as they run to one favorite grown-up and slight another.

Why do you teach? Is it for the praise of the children, the pastor, the parents? Is it to impress a friend? Is it out of a sense that God will love you more? Is it because you'd feel guilty if you weren't doing something in the church, and teaching seemed better than cleaning toilets? Is it to show off your knowledge of the Bible?

Several years ago I read an article asking teachers to examine their motives. The article stressed that the teacher needed to stop teaching if his motives were less than pure. I wouldn't say that. None of us has totally pure motives for doing anything. Our sin nature infects everything we touch, everything we breathe on. A sense of gratitude to God, for instance, can easily turn into a sense that somehow what we do for Him is paying off a debt. We can turn affection for children into idolatry and end up teaching more because we love boys and girls than because we love God. We can move beyond a sense of responsibility into a sense of tedious duty or a resentment of those who seem to do less in the church than we do. We can even justify ourselves when our bad motives far outweigh our good, by looking at other people and trying to figure out why *they* volunteered.

Wrong motives can easily strip away not only our reward but our pleasure, our effectiveness, our humility, and our gratitude toward God. They plug up the places where God's grace should shine out in our lives, leading others to Him when they see our joy and our love overflowing in service. God does not need you—you're more expendable than the greasy-haired sixteen-year-old employee at Burger King who calls in sick twice a week. He uses you by choice—for His glory and your joy.

Part of keeping a proper perspective is a correct view of oneself. I often take myself too seriously, thinking that my perspective is the only possible one or that if I don't do something it won't get done. Teaching children has helped me learn to relax, to laugh at myself, to develop a more humorous view of the world, to be more teachable, and to say "I'm sorry" when I need to.

Why do you teach? Is it for love of God and His Word, the children, their families, and your church? Or is it for love of the praise of man or the good feeling of your own conscience?

For Thought

1. Sit quietly before God, and ask Him to reveal any false motives in your teaching. Confess them to Him as sin, and ask Him to keep you sensitive in those areas.

2. What are some good reasons to teach children? Pray that God will instill a passion for those reasons deeper in your heart.

31

YOUR COFFEE BREAK: A WORD OF ENCOURAGEMENT

Therefore, my beloved brethren, be steadfast, immovable,
always abounding in the work of the Lord, knowing that
your labor is not in vain in the Lord.

(1 CORINTHIANS 15:58)

One hour a week is all most of us have with the children we teach. Throw in an occasional class get-together, home visit, or phone call, and it's still a small fraction of a child's week. What can we really teach in one hour Sunday morning or ninety minutes Wednesday night?

I'm encouraged when I remember that God can take my small efforts and expand them for His purposes. After all, one of the world's most famous preachers, Paul, referred to the "foolishness of preaching" (1 Corinthians 1:21 KJV). Our efforts require faithfulness, but it is God who "gives the increase" (1 Corinthians 3:7).

I think back to the adults who had the most influence on me when I was a child, and I know some would be surprised to hear that they affected my life at all. I don't even remember all their names. But God used assorted people besides my parents in various ways to help me love Him and His church and His people. Many times such love has been hard, but the pattern was set in childhood, and it's hard to break now.

A few years ago I observed a teacher who continually used big words far over the heads of her third-grade students. She also spoke in a monotone, and she probably spoke for too long at a time. I was surprised when I saw how much the kids liked her. I was surprised, that is, until I saw how much this dear old lady loved her children. She even had them over to her house for dinner after church, two each week. Could she have used some teaching pointers? Yes. But other, "better" teachers in the church could have learned at least as much from her.

When teaching a semester of college English, I asked the students to write about someone in their lives, other than a parent or boyfriend or girlfriend, who had been significant in some way. At least three students wrote about their youth pastors. One girl wrote about someone a little less obvious—an old lady in a nursing home. The student had tagged along with two friends who went to the nursing home, and the woman quietly asked her to come back by herself another time. She returned several times. She says she was a teenager who dressed in clothing other adults usually thought rebellious, so she wasn't well accepted at church. But one old lady loved her in a small way, and that little bit of love made a big impression on a young girl.

Children are masters of the small detail. Little bits of love, offhand comments, a godly decision made while an unseen child watches—it's hard to know what God can use as you teach children. But God loves your boys and girls even more than you do. Your faithfulness is important to Him. He sees it. He knows the hard times. And He can use you in your students' lives, sometimes in spite of yourself.

For Thought

1. What adults made a significant or meaningful influence on your life when you were a child? Why?

2. How has God used a child to encourage you recently?

PART 5

UNDERSTANDING AND PREPARING THE LESSON

How has God worked in human history? What is His goal? What is His essential nature, His character? What is the nature of man? What are his basic needs? How does the death of Jesus Christ fit into the picture? How do we know what is true? These are only some of the questions we answer in learning to think biblically.

—GLADYS HUNT,
Honey for a Child's Heart (Grand Rapids: Zondervan, 1989), 95.

32

FIFTEEN MINUTES TO PREPARE

Study to shew thyself approved unto God, a
workman that needeth not to be ashamed,
rightly dividing the word of truth.

(2 TIMOTHY 2:15 KJV)

Before beginning his message, the chapel speaker apologized for it. He explained that he had been asked to speak (to more than a thousand college students) only fifteen minutes before, when the scheduled speaker had been unable to come. Talk about pressure!

I thought back to a casual comment I'd made to an adult when I was a teenager and a new Sunday school teacher. "My lesson was kind of short this week. I had to go to bed early last night, so I didn't really get time to study."

Over time, my preparation time had slowly shortened. The first few weeks I taught, I raced into my bedroom after school and opened the teacher's guide. I knew my responsibility was great, and the privilege felt great, too. But other things had crowded in, until I heard myself explaining that my preparation time had been pushed back to the half hour before bed Saturday night—and that even that had been canceled the night before when Mom sent me to bed early. As I verbalized what I had done, I heard myself and realized how far I had come.

I'd like to say that now I always start lesson preparation after church Sunday so I'll be ready for the next week. In fact, I usually don't. But the best hours of teaching have been those times that were backed with preparation that began the previous Monday or Tuesday. When I fully know my material and don't have to even glance at my notes, I can interact more fully with my students. I'm more open to their immediate needs, more able to be flexible, and—most important—more open to the Holy Spirit's guidance as He teaches me.

Ed Dunlop (yes, he's my big brother) lists six "reasons for lesson preparation early in the week":

1. You are able to evaluate the previous lesson accurately.
2. The needs and problems of your students are fresh in your mind.
3. You have plenty of time for proper study.

4. You are able to meditate on the lesson all week.
5. You have time to gather needed material.
6. You have time to become acquainted with current pupil needs.[1]

The first time you look through a lesson does not have to be time-consuming. I usually begin by reading the relevant Scripture passage(s) once. If an idea for teaching comes to mind, I write it down, but I don't really dwell on it. Often, the second time I read the passage, an illustration or application will come up. I then have time later in the week to read the verses again and see if it truly fits. I may read some of the text before and after the story I'll be teaching or read the same story from other places in the Bible. After I have read the passage a couple of times on different nights, I then look at my teacher's guide to see if it gives any other ideas.

By that time, I know the passage well enough that I can see if the teacher's guide emphasizes its writer's pet idea rather than what Scripture teaches. I also can see whether some ideas it suggests would work well for me and my class. I pull together visual aids, review activities, pre-session activities, Bible memory verses or songs, and other parts of the class hour. Eventually I make brief notes of the lesson on an index card, which I put in my Bible so that I can refresh my memory before class and can glance at it if I lose my place during class.

By the end of the week, the story has gathered shape. A possible reason for the character's action may have come to mind. I may have thought of other books I have that explain cultural details from that time period. Something in another book I have read during the week or a conversation I have had may have suggested a method that will help me teach. But the methods and illustrations won't overwhelm the story itself, because reading it several times from the Bible has helped me to know it rather well.

Lord, speak to me that I may speak
In living echoes of Thy tone
As Thou hast sought, so let me seek
The erring children lost and lone.

Oh! teach me, Lord, that I may teach
The precious things Thou dost impart;
And wing my words, that they may reach
The hidden depths of many a heart.

—Frances R. Havergal

Note

1. Ed Dunlop, *"How Do I Get These Kids to Listen?" Practical Ways to Gain and Hold Attention in the Classroom* (Murfreesboro, Tenn.: Sword of the Lord, 1997), 17.

For Evaluation

1. When do you usually start your lesson preparation? What factors of your teaching would be improved if you started earlier?

2. Look at your schedule. What is a realistic day, early in the week, to begin preparing next week's lesson?

33

LESSON PLANNING
Part One: Teaching
What the Bible Teaches

We will not hide them from their children, telling to the generation to come the praises of the Lord, and His strength and His wonderful works that He has done. . . . that they should make them known to their children; that the generation to come might know them, the children who would be born, that they may arise and declare them to their children.

(PSALM 78:4, 6)

A white-whiskered, plump grandfather stands surrounded by dozens of animals neatly lined up in pairs as they approach the ramp to a large boat. Later, a pretty dove, then a rainbow, will grace the deep blue sky. For good reason, the story of Noah's ark, simplified to cuteness, appeals to children. Thumb through just about any catalog of children's books, and you will probably find at least one book telling this particular biblical story. But usually the story has been reworked into a cute secular myth.

I have a copy of a children's picture-book version of the story that mentions God only once, in a passing reference on the first page. ("One day God told [Noah] that a great flood was coming." Noah reassures his wife, "But I know what to do.") The book is part of a series of twenty popular children's tales, including "Chicken Little," "Jack and the Beanstalk," and "The Ugly Duckling." The fact that Noah's ark is the only story on the list that even claims to be true probably occurs to few readers. I have even seen the story used to advance environmentalism—sweet old Noah, saving all those innocent animals. Of course, those uses presuppose the tale is not literally true.

Such retellings not only do not include God (at least not in any significant way), but they also do not have judgment, sin, death, God's covenant never again to destroy the earth by water, grace—or any meaningful purpose. Read the story in Genesis 6–9 carefully, and you may wonder why even Christians consider it mainly a pretty story for children. Parts of it are definitely not rated "G."

It is of little more than passing interest that secular publishers have reworked a story from the Bible and in the process diluted or eliminated its meaning. What is far more significant is how often Christian teachers unconsciously do the same thing with Scripture.

Look at the following chart of a few stories commonly taught to children. In the first column, I have listed the story; in the second, what is usually taught from it; in the third, what I believe the Bible actually emphasizes. You might want to cover the third column and see if you can think of the Bible's emphasis. What you were taught as a child probably focused on the second column, and what we are taught tends to linger in our minds.

STORY	WHAT WE TEACH	WHAT THE BIBLE TEACHES
Jesus feeding 5,000 (John 6)[1]	importance of sharing, giving to God	Christ's power
Jonah and the fish	not being prejudiced, or obeying God	God's mercy (to Ninevites and Jonah)
Joshua and the Israelites at Jericho (Joshua 6)	Joshua's obedience or battle strategy	God's power
Shadrach, Meshach, and Abednego (Daniel 3)	the men's courage	God's faithfulness

The *points* of the second column are in some cases found in the stories. But are they the *purpose* of each story's presence in Holy Scripture? As pastor and author Michael Horton likes to say, the Bible is not *Aesop's Fables* or *The Book of Virtues*. It was not given to teach us how to be good or to be nice people. It was given that we might know God.

Without the third column, your students are unlikely to have any motivation for the morality in the second, even if they do choose to imitate the actions of those godly men or avoid imitating their bad deeds. Such imitation will be based on an "ought to" motivation divorced from a loving response to God. Teaching a virtue without its proper response to God's character may bring legalistic obedience, guilt, or apathy. The church already has enough of all three.

Teaching courage, for example, without the foundation of God's trustworthiness disconnects courage from faith in a God who protects us. The story of Shadrach, Meshach, and Abednego deals with courage in the face of persecution, not with mere macho bravado. Courage during persecution may seem an irrelevant topic for children. But not only is the fact that the Bible teaches it an important enough reason for teaching it, but also any child who mentions God in public schools today truly needs supernatural courage.

Too often our question is, "What would I like to teach from this passage?" But the most important question, if we understand the Bible's focus to be knowing God, is, "What does this passage tell us about God?"

John H. Walton, Laurie Bailey, and Craig Williford explain one reason that creating our own application can be problematic:

> If the Bible is used only as a jump-off point for one's own objectives, the Bible's authority is being bypassed, because if a passage is not being used to teach what the Bible is teaching, the teacher stands only in his/her own authority. Too much of today's curriculum teaches only with human authority rather than with the authority of God.[2]

So let's look at our chart again, reworking it for a more biblical focus:

STORY	WHAT THE BIBLE TEACHES	AN APPROPRIATE RESPONSE
Jesus feeding 5,000	Christ's power	reverence, thankfulness
Jonah and the fish	God's mercy (to the Ninevites and to Jonah)	obedient witnessing
Joshua and the Israelites at Jericho	God's power	trust, obedience
Shadrach, Meshach, and Abednego	God's faithfulness	trust

If you use published curriculum, take time to evaluate how much of its emphasis is on God. How much is on teaching morality without the proper foundation of who God is and what He has done? Does the curriculum recognize the fact that even our obedience comes through His power? Does it teach what the Bible teaches—and do you?

Notes

1. This example comes from Gary Bredfeldt and Larry Richards, *Creative Bible Teaching* (Chicago: Moody, 1997), 203. The concepts in this chapter evolved from the challenge in *Creative Bible Teaching* to teach only what the Bible teaches.
2. John H. Walton, Laurie Bailey, and Craig Williford, "Bible-Based Curricula and the Crisis of Scriptural Authority," *Christian Education Journal*, vol. 13, no. 3, 85.

For Action

1. Write down the Scripture references for the next two or three lessons you will teach. Look up each passage, and jot down what you believe to be the Bible's focus.

2. Now jot down what your curriculum places as the focus for those same lessons. If the difference is pronounced, it is particularly important to deal with Scripture before you look at the teacher's guide as you prepare each week.

EVALUATING PUBLISHED CURRICULUM

	Avoid	Use Cautiously	Look for
Vision of Scripture	lessons jump back and forth between OT and NT rather than following the Bible's own storyline by having at least a few consecutive lessons; doesn't treat the Bible as literally true	oversimplifies Bible stories as though the enjoyment of a story is its primary reason for telling it; consistently looks only at well-known Bible stories; makes up a lot of story details to make the story more interesting	understanding of the Gospel, along with belief by the writers that children can be saved; close attention to following what Scripture actually says (not "spicing up" the story to make it more interesting); gives more background to aid understanding, such as customs of the day or connection to a previous story
Application of Scripture	applies lessons with activities and games that have no clear connection to the lesson	strays too far from Scripture in making its application (this curriculum can still be used by the discerning teacher if otherwise the content is good; just don't use the suggested application)	looks very closely at why the story is told in Scripture, particularly at how it applies to God's salvation story, then looks at what we can learn from it or how we can apply it today
Focus of Teaching time	relies on videos to do the teaching; doesn't have a clear lesson from Scripture every week, but sometimes substitutes a skit or a "learning activity" on some social issue	de-emphasizes the lesson portion of the hour	uses the Bible heavily, with everything in the hour going back to Scripture; attempts to build in students a growing knowledge of the Bible and increasing love for God
Supplementary Material (pictures, games, songs, maps, etc.)	seem to be included for kid-appeal rather than their connection to the lesson	seem dated or old; made for wrong age	each part of the hour reinforces the Scripture with review, helps to memory, or application
Understanding of Children	treats children as spectators to be entertained or lectured rather than as people to be taught	curriculum that is written for older or younger children than the ones you teach	has a sense of children's responsibility before God and their accountability to adult authority; understands and explains the unique traits of the age group

The Teacher's Role	limited to being a facilitator guiding a learning process	undefined role; person who should go through material and do everything exactly as instructed, with no room for teacher's own personality or the guidance of the Word	humbly teaching children, with responsibility for and authority over students and responsibility to God for appropriate teaching

Note

1. Most children's curriculum is set up roughly like this: January Theme—God's Power. Week one: Jonah and the Fish; Week two: Joshua at Jericho; Week three: Jesus Raises Lazarus; Week four: David Defeats Goliath. The problem, first, is that the writers usually only use God's power as a cute ploy to tie the lessons together, but they really emphasize something else in the story. The second problem is that kids are taught the Bible as a series of disjointed stories. Stories need not always be taught chronologically, but could your average eight-year-old Sunday school child say whether Moses or Jesus was born first? Disconnected lessons may be stimulating in themselves, but they do not lead to a growing knowledge of the Bible. As a result, most adult Christians do not have an understanding of the flow, history, or even theology of the Bible. Instead they have at best a disjointed awareness of the Bible's message and its content.

LESSON PLANNING
Part Two: Two
Important Questions

*It is written in the prophets, "And they shall all be taught
by God." Therefore everyone who has heard and learned
from the Father comes to Me.*

(JOHN 6:45)

In many Sunday school lessons the Bible character, not God, becomes the hero of the story. If the teacher is telling the story of Daniel and the lions, the student finds the narrative exciting, and he silently adds Daniel to his list of heroes. If he believes that the story is actually true, it seems even more exciting. Then, at the end of the lesson, the teacher may suggest an application. She may emphasize that children should "be brave enough to pray to God even if other people don't like it."

If the student's mind is full of Daniel's heroic actions rather than God's trustworthy protection, he may obey as a response to the teacher, or in imitation of the hero whose story he has heard, not as a response to who God is. That moves God from His place as the center of life, and especially the center of Scripture, to a postscript. (Daniel was brave. P.S. God came through.) Beyond that, when the child actually does pray boldly in his public school lunchroom, if other kids make fun of him he will probably decide Daniel was braver than he is, and he will stop praying. An application that lacks the proper motivation is thus not biblical and not strong enough to fit real life.

In the last chapter I emphasized that a Bible lesson needs to start with the Bible's starting point. Since the Bible teaches us about God, what a passage tells us about *Him* is primary. But the Bible also shows us ourselves. So the two questions most basic when preparing a lesson are: What does this passage say about God? and What does this passage say about man? (See the reproducible lesson-planning chart, which follows this chapter and uses these two questions to help you prepare the lesson.)

What does this passage say about God? Which of His attributes are taught or illustrated? Does the passage emphasize God's holiness and refusal to be in the presence of sin? Does it focus on His mercy? His power? What does it say about His actions? Does it speak of His creation, His offer of salvation, His gentleness in dealing with the weak, His wrath when confronting blasphemy?

What does this passage say about man? Characters in Scripture show us some ways people can respond to God and what happens as a result. Here is where the application comes through. Was the main character (or characters) a believer or an unbeliever? If he was an unbeliever, how did God show who He is (for example, His dealing with Pharaoh during the ten plagues)? If he was a believer, was his response to God good or bad? A study of the life of David shows a strong cause-effect. Sometimes he acted wisely, sometimes sinfully. His repentance brought God's mercy, yet his sin had consequences. Even when he was obedient, life was not easy, but God faithfully trained him for his significant role in Israel's history.

Once you've answered those two questions, you can look at the details of a passage and note *what other questions* the passage asks and answers. What genre is the passage written in (is it a story, a poem, a letter giving instruction, or something else)? Who besides the main character(s) is involved in this tale? Why? What happened before and after the incident told in this passage? Where did this take place? When did it happen? (Children need to know whether it was before or after Jesus lived, and they need to know roughly how it fits into the Bible narrative.) What other passages of Scripture refer to this incident or this person?

After you are familiar with the Scripture account and what it teaches, see whether you can tell it in your own words. When you can do that, it's time to see how the teacher's guide can help the rest of your preparation.

The teacher's guide can often help you:

- understand Bible times
- understand how the children are likely to respond
- tell the story using words children can understand and relate to
- apply the story
- plan other creative activities that reinforce the lesson
- reinforce the lesson by suggesting an appropriate memory verse
- illustrate the lesson with appropriate visual aids

But you cannot afford to read the teacher's guide instead of reading the Bible. Since many guides suggest main points to the lesson that are different from what Scripture teaches, *always* read the passage first and figure out answers to the first two questions (God and man) before you read the teacher's guide.

If you are dissatisfied with the way your curriculum deals with Scripture, two publishers whose curriculum is worth looking at are Child Evangelism Fellowship and New Tribes Mission.[1] But whatever curriculum you work with, the Bible needs to be your main resource.

Note

1. To contact these ministries: Child Evangelism Fellowship, P.O. Box 348, Warrenton, MO 63383; New Tribes Mission, 1000 E. First Street, Sanford, FL 32771-1487, (407) 323-3430.

For Action

1. Look at the Lesson Planning Form on the next page. Read the passage you will be teaching next week, and answer the questions on a separate sheet of paper or a photocopy of the chart.

2. Look at your teacher's guide, and find answers to some of the "other questions" listed on p. 120.

LESSON PLANNING FORM

Scripture Passage _____ Lesson _____

1. What does this story/passage emphasize about God? (His attributes and/or actions)

2. What does this passage say about man? (What did the person/people do right or wrong in response to God? What can we learn from this action or response? What does it say to the saved child? the unsaved child?)

3. What happens in this story? Summarize in four or five points.

4. What is the main point of the lesson? (e.g., "God can take care of a person who trusts Him.")

5. What is the application of this lesson? (e.g., "I can trust God when I am afraid of people who don't like me.")

6. What might be a good small-group activity or application exercise?

7. What words or concepts may need to be defined?

8. Is there any background or setting that will need to be explained?

9. What visual aids or other tools could help me teach this lesson?

This chart is taken from Cheryl Dunlop, *Follow Me As I Follow Christ* (Chicago: Moody, 2000) and is used by permission.

35

WHEN IS APPLICATION OF SCRIPTURE DANGEROUS?

Are you so foolish? Having begun in the Spirit,
are you now being made perfect by the flesh?

(GALATIANS 3:3)

Just about every resource on Christian teaching emphasizes that the application of truth is essential. Without application, students will eventually have much knowledge about Scripture, but their actions will not match what they know. They may be hypocrites, or at least they will have the potential to be proud of what they know without ever learning that what we know should affect who we are.

This is true. But the danger of applying every lesson by encouraging student action is that a child may subtly pick up something we do not intend to teach: that Christianity is defined by something we *do*. It was exactly this misperception that Paul was attacking when he said, "Are you so foolish? Having begun in the Spirit, are you now being made perfect by the flesh?" (Galatians 3:3).

Most Christian adults could probably list "the rules of Christianity" easier than they could discuss biblical content or give the meaning behind the Bible's teachings. Curriculum that emphasizes application of biblical truth often points out the need for a teacher to give students a measurable action: Fill out this chart by checking off every day this week that you read the Bible. Tell one classmate about Christ this week. Invite a friend to church. And so on.

If a teacher consistently makes such an application every week, would he have remarkably godly children at the end of a year as a result? Probably not. More likely he would have a mixture of the following: (a) an unsaved child vainly trying to do as many of the "good" things he has heard as he can in order to make God happy; (b) a Christian child who does a fairly good job of following "the rules" and who is thus learning legalism and Christian pride; (c) a Christian child who is discouraged because the Christian life seems too complicated; (d) a child who tries to do the applications each week to make the teacher happy or to earn prizes; and (e) a child who tunes out everything except the story.

I'm not saying applications should be downplayed; the Bible is quite clear that we should be doers and not merely hearers. The problem is the danger that students may hear the application but miss the truth behind it (who God is, what He has done, and how we should respond to Him). Is there a place for letting students be stunned with the glory of God and allowing them to walk out *worshiping* rather than *doing?*

We need to get kids into Scripture and get Scripture into them; yet their response must be to God Himself, not to us and not to a legalistic "biblical rule-following." I'm not saying we obey some "personal revelation" rather than Scripture, merely that it's easy to follow every jot and tittle and thus believe ourselves to be good Christians. But the Law of God condemns; we cannot keep it, and we cannot be "good Christians" by trying. If a pupil comes to know God, changed behavior will follow, but it will be a response of humble gratitude to God, not a vain attempt to keep the Law and make God happy.

Scripture is supposed to change our lives, but must every passage have an immediate application? If we insist on it, are we teaching pragmatism rather than Christianity? Are we teaching that the purpose of Scripture is to help make our lives more organized or more moral? Isn't it supposed to get beneath our skin and into our minds and hearts, where it subtly works to change our attitudes and actions? Shouldn't our most frequent response to Scripture be to recognize how great God is, bringing us first to worship and only then to action as a *response?*

We have too many young Christians bored with Christianity. Many others see it as a list of rules they can either accept or reject. The church isn't even passing on facts very well; the rate of biblical illiteracy is at an all-time high. But most important, we are failing dramatically at a bigger point: We are not experiencing or passing on a passion for God.

I read recently that teachers should select only memory verses that have immediate application to students' lives. I agree that such verses are important, but we ought not limit Scripture to immediately relevant truths. Do we, for example, teach children that marriage should be permanent? Do we teach about the Trinity? missions? the inspiration of Scripture? the nature of the church? the Second Coming? Much of the Bible doesn't seem "relevant" (especially to children), but neither is the Bible a how-to manual or a twelve-step book. It's the Word of God. God promises it will not return void, so shouldn't we sow some seed that may not bear fruit for decades at the same time we tell children what God wants for them today?

Another danger is that lessons are too often applied as though every child in the room were a Christian. The story of the woman at the well speaks to the unsaved child, who needs Christ, as much as to the saved child who needs to witness to others, and your class probably contains boys and girls in both categories.

I'm afraid many of us were reared with truth being "applied" and commanded before we even really saw the truth itself. Many adults spend their whole lives *doing* without really knowing God. I can't picture anything more beautiful than a class of children who know, worship, and obey God—in that order. In the next chapter we'll look at obeying Him, the proper use of application.

For Further Study

1. Study Romans 8; Galatians 3:23–25. Why did God give the Law? Did He expect us to be able to keep it?

2. If you can, read through the entire book of Romans during the next week. The Christian is called to obedience. What does that mean? What is the place of the Law in a Christian's life?

36

APPLICATION
THAT FITS

*As you have therefore received Christ Jesus
the Lord, so walk in Him, rooted and built
up in Him and established in the faith,
as you have been taught, abounding in it
with thanksgiving.*

(COLOSSIANS 2:6–7)

Most Christians have known people who could quote whole chapters of Scripture and who seem to know where to find in the Bible the answer to any question, yet who have still fallen into deliberate patterns of sin. Why? Living the Christian life takes more than knowledge. In fact, it takes more than knowledge and resolve to do the right thing.

To transform a child—or adult—into the image of Christ takes both the Holy Spirit's work in that individual's life and the person's own willingness to choose Christ over himself. But the Holy Spirit doesn't usually communicate directly today. He uses the truth of Scripture and applies it. He speaks to the conscience, reminding us of what we already know to be true. For the Holy Spirit to have material to teach, the believer must read the Word or have it in his heart. The human teacher thus must teach the Word in order to implant in the child love for God, knowledge of Scripture, and the desire to do what is right.

It is generally understood that scriptural truth can be divided into three parts for the purpose of a lesson:

(1) **observation**—what happened
(2) **interpretation**—why we need to know what happened (how it is important to the overall story of Scripture)
(3) **application**—what it means to our lives today

Unfortunately, it is remarkably easy to jump from step one to step three without recognizing the missed step. For example, I've seen Jesus' temptation by Satan taught without any focus on why it was significant that Christ defeated him. Most of the lesson time was spent on what the lesson might say to the children and why they should respond with Scripture when they are tempted. Application that ignores Scripture's point is merely moralistic teaching, not biblical teaching, no matter how well-intentioned. *Why* Scripture tells us a certain story or a certain truth is much more important than *what* we can do with that information, and what we can do with that information should always be based on why it is told in Scripture.

It's one thing to know what truth needs to be applied to our lives and our students' lives. But knowing truth still is not applying truth in action. Application can be a response of the mind (knowing, memorizing truth), of the heart (responding in worship or sorrow), of the will (repentance), or of the body (doing). Here are a few lessons from Scripture, broken into the three parts. Note that not only does each passage list truth to apply, but each has at least one suggested practical application.

Story (observation)	Truth (interpretation)	Relevance Today (truth to apply)	Action Step (application)
Cain's killing of Abel (Genesis 4:1–16): God gave clear commands for sacrifice; Cain disobeyed, but Abel obeyed; God warned Cain; Cain disregarded God and killed Abel	God: God is holy and must be approached correctly Man: Cain, trying to come to God in his own way, completely lost sight of God Himself	We must come to God only in the way He has declared Unsaved child: salvation comes only through Christ Saved child: correct worship	Unsaved child: accept Christ Saved child: to the best of your ability, follow along in the worship service so that you can worship God with other believers
Daniel in the lions' den (Daniel 6): Daniel's contemporaries were jealous; they had a law passed that requests had to be made only of the king; Daniel continued regular prayers; Daniel was thrown into the lions' den; God kept Daniel alive	God: God's ability and supernatural protection Man: Daniel obeyed God and trusted Him rather than seeking his own protection	We can trust God to take care of us; when we obey Him, the consequences are His responsibility. It's OK to stand alone in a crowd	For Christian children in public schools (or those who regularly interact with unbelievers in other settings): resolving before God to let Him handle any ridicule that comes from standing up for Him
Satan tempting Christ (Matthew 4:1–11): Jesus after His baptism went into the desert, where He fasted and prayed for 40 days; Satan came and tempted Him three times; Christ resisted all the temptations, then was strengthened by angels	God: the Trinity; the deity of Christ Man: Christ in the flesh resisting the temptations that the "first Adam" succumbed to Satan: his evil character, the danger of listening to him; his power thwarted	We need to believe Jesus is who He said He is. We can take comfort in Christ's strength when we are tempted; following His example, we need to fight temptation with Scripture and turning Satan over to Christ	Mind: recognize Jesus' deity Heart: trust in Him Will: memorize Scripture Body: obey God and use Scripture to resist temptations to disobey (What temptations do your kids deal with?)

The concepts developed under the "truth (interpretation)" column are another way of looking at the questions developed in chapter 34. What is the text's *intended teaching*? That is proper interpretation.

Once you know what the passage says (its general truths), you can determine what it means for people today—particularly yourself and your students. That is proper application.

Column four in the chart makes application specific, rather than ending a lesson with a vague "We should trust God." You could ask your students to tell you in what situations they might need to trust God, then have them pray quietly. They might memorize a relevant Scripture, then take home a written copy of it. Or you could have each child draw a picture on a piece of paper on which you have written, "God protected Daniel when Daniel admitted he knew God. God can take care of me too." One-on-one discussions, inside or outside class, provide wonderful opportunities to apply truth to an individual child's specific circumstances.

May your teaching be empowered by the Holy Spirit as He implants the Word firmly in the hearts of your students.

For Action

1. Make a chart with the four columns used above.

2. In column one, list the next five lessons you will teach, with spaces between each one. Spend some time reading the Scripture passages and filling out the other columns (in pencil, so you can work with them once you start doing more involved study for that particular lesson). You will probably want to leave column four blank for now. (Column four should list ideas relevant to your own class, not general ones.) Remember the previous chapter—you should not apply a lesson just to apply it but teach what the passage was meant to teach, whatever the required response.

37

TEACHING BY ASKING QUESTIONS

He said to them, "But who do you say
that I am?" And Peter answered and
said to Him, "You are the Christ."

(MARK 8:29)

Show Me a denarius. Whose image and inscription does it have?" "What is written in the law? What is your reading of it?" "Who touched Me?" "So which of these three do you think was neighbor to him who fell among the thieves?"

Scripture says of Christ that He didn't need anyone to tell Him about man, because He knew what was in man. When Jesus was only twelve, He amazed learned teachers of the Law with His answers to their questions. When Satan tempted Him in the desert, He showed that He knew what Scripture really meant. So why did He ask people so many questions? *Because it's one of the most effective ways to teach.*

Jesus wasn't asking out of ignorance or to gain information. He wasn't even asking questions in order to get to know people better. He asked questions to make people think (Luke 6:9), to challenge them to action (Luke 10:36), to point out their inconsistencies (Mark 11:29–30), to make them understand their own ignorance or their need (Mark 9:33), or to arouse their curiosity before He answered His own question with a story or further teaching (Luke 24:14–32).

What can good questions do for the teacher of children?

1. They can show us what our students actually heard or what they remember, allowing for review and correction of false assumptions and also allowing us to evaluate how effectively we have taught.
2. They force students to think, and they make them pay attention.
3. They show the students that we care whether they learn and that we want to hear their voices, not just our own.
4. They involve students in the lesson and allow for some flexibility.
5. They allow students to practice putting what they believe into words in a supportive atmosphere.

6. They challenge students to think through the implications of what they have heard.

7. They allow for restatement of what the students have learned and thus help the other students review. (Of course, the teacher must be willing to gently correct false answers.)

8. They help the teacher learn effective ways of communicating with students as he hears how they word the truths he has taught.

9. They can open up class discussion.

10. They can encourage children to ask their own questions, which can provide an opportunity to look at the Bible together.

All of that assumes the questions you ask are good ones. Some questions ask merely for easy facts: What was the name of the man swallowed by the fish? Some probe a little deeper, though still looking for facts: What did God tell Jonah to do? Deeper still: Why did Jonah get on a ship going the wrong way? What did God want Jonah to learn? Each kind of question is important, but in general the more thought-provoking, the better.

One effective method for using questions is a review game.[1] Games can take place at the end of a class period, reviewing that day's lesson, or they can be done at the beginning of a period, covering the lesson from the week before or several lessons. They can be as simple as two teams (boys against girls), a ladder or a tic-tac-toe board on the chalkboard, and a few questions. They can be as complicated as game boards with scorekeepers and timed answers. Questions should be written ahead of time so that you won't have to waste class time thinking of them and so that one team can't tell you, "You're giving them all the easy questions!" Kenny was an eight-year-old who resisted obedience, yet we developed a rapport over the year I taught him, and he learned to love Bible games. I did not use one every week, but Kenny's first question each week was, "Are we going to play a game today?"

Some children can feel left out of a Bible game, since inevitably some students are a lot better at it than others. Used carelessly, review games can teach students that Bible facts are equivalent to Trivial Pursuit®. Minimize those problems with creativity (such as allowing each child to answer only two questions), by asking a few open-ended questions that don't require one precise answer, and by asking follow-up questions you can direct to a child who doesn't speak up much but who knows the answer.

Particularly when questions are used outside the structure of a game, it can be valuable to ask questions that more than one child can answer. Such questions can get a discussion going. For example, "Why should the people who lived when Jesus lived have known He was God?" or, "What would you say to a person who says he is good enough to go to heaven?"

And now I have a question for you: What are three things that some good questions can add to your teaching?

Note

1. For dozens of review games of all sorts (including overhead projector games and many other varieties), see Ed Dunlop, *Mouse on a Mission: 54 Bible Review Games to Reinforce Your Lesson* (Murfreesboro, Tenn.: Sword of the Lord, 1999).

For Action

1. Look through the Gospels to find three additional questions Jesus asked people. Why did He ask each one?

2. Look over the lesson you taught last week. From it, write ten questions, making sure that some of them go beyond the surface. Now look for a way to incorporate the questions into your upcoming lesson.

PART 6

TEACHING THE LESSON

Is the parallel society of the Christian community preserving its history and its idioms by telling and retelling its stories in the presence of its children? Similarly, are we singing the songs of the alternative community for the sake of our children's memory, to preserve the fertility of our offspring's faith?

—MARVA J. DAWN,
Is It a Lost Cause? Having the Heart of God for the Church's Children (Grand Rapids: Eerdmans, 1997), 122.

38

COMMUNICATING ON A CHILD'S LEVEL

*But sanctify the Lord God in your hearts, and always be ready
to give a defense to everyone who asks you a reason for the hope
that is in you, with meekness and fear.*

(1 PETER 3:15)

Let's explore the pedagogical, sociological, and ecclesiastical ramifications of utilizing incomprehensible polysyllabic verbiage. After all, lucidity elicits comprehension, but undefined terms cause students' eyes to glaze over.

Huh? What was that again?

That was my opening paragraph in a teacher-training session I'd prepared about communicating on a child's level. Assuming that it would take just about that long to completely lose the attention of my student teachers, at that point I stopped and yelled, "You're not listening!" Then I turned to a teacher who had agreed to help me and asked her, "Renee, what did I just say?" The obvious answer is "I don't know."

I have sat in on many classes taught by well-meaning teachers who use undefined big words with children. I wonder as I listen how many discipline problems could be avoided simply by making sure students *understand* what we say. If students don't understand, they are unlikely to listen and even less likely to learn.

It takes experience to learn how to communicate with boys and girls. It's hard to avoid the dual extremes of talking down to them and talking over their heads. But since our main task is *communicating,* and since *what* we communicate defines us as Bible teachers, it's worth some effort to learn how to use child-friendly vocabulary.

I use a few tricks to help me. Sometimes, when I use a word I'm not sure kids know, I ask *them* to define it. That tells me whether they know the term, it allows me to correct misunderstandings, and it gets them involved. It also helps me stay on their level of understanding when I define words if I listen to what they say when *they* give the definitions.

Do you communicate clearly? A camp preacher told junior-age boys and girls they needed to ask Jesus into their hearts, without defining what that means. He spent twenty minutes on how necessary it is to ask Jesus into one's heart. But he didn't actually present the Gospel, because he didn't talk about sin, the Cross, or forgiveness. He did tell the children that those who have not asked Jesus into their hearts will go to hell . . . and he defined hell much more vividly than he had defined salvation.

Several of the girls in my cabin were trembling or asking worried questions when we left that evening service. Many of them had spoken quite confidently of Christ earlier in the week, so I knew we probably had a communication problem more than a spiritual problem. Instead of going directly to the campfire as we were supposed to do (a campfire that might be quite scary after a detailed description of hell), I herded the girls into the cabin and attempted to do damage repair.

I started by saying, "Some of you asked me if it's true what he said—that people who don't ask Jesus into their hearts go to hell. Yes, it's true. But let me explain what that means. First, there are a lot of different ways to say it. 'Asking Jesus to forgive your sins' and 'believing on Jesus' and 'becoming a Christian' are all different ways of saying the same thing. If you know you're a sinner, you believe that Jesus died on the cross for your sin, and you have trusted Him to forgive your sin, you don't need to be afraid of hell." Some of the girls relaxed visibly, and I was able to answer their questions before we headed out to the campfire.

As you prepare to teach next week, pay attention to your language. Are you using words that the children may not understand? Are you using concepts that may be too advanced for the age group? A general rule of teaching is not to use abstract concepts for kids below junior age. Jesus is described in Scripture as the "bread of life" and a "gift from God," but those terms are beyond the comprehension of most young children. That is one reason stories work so well for boys and girls. It's easier for them to understand who Jesus is if they can picture Him as a person. Jesus came to die, but He also came so that we would know what God is like. He put flesh on theology. Stories about Him do the same thing for children.

Listen to the way kids talk with each other. Sit in on a class taught by an effective teacher. Read books written for children of the age you teach. Notice what words your curriculum uses. Don't be afraid to use big words, especially words that are important to the Christian faith—just be sure your students know what they mean.

For Action

1. Develop a definition for each of the following terms, using words and concepts that would be clear to the students you teach: faithful, grace, holy, save, repent, sin, Gospel.

2. Look at the material you are using in next week's class: the lesson itself, the memory verse, songs, etc. Decide how you will define any words that may be unclear to your students.

39

TELLING A
BIBLE STORY
Part One: Some Guidelines

Come, you children, listen to me; I will teach you the fear of the Lord.

(PSALM 34:11)

To tell a story well, you must be thoroughly acquainted with it. (Do you have to refer to notes when you tell the events of your day?) Of course, your class's familiarity with the story will also affect how you tell it. The more familiar the story already is to your listeners, the more creative you must be in telling it, *but creativity does not mean falsification.* Certain details not given in Scripture, such as many of the customs of Israelite families, may be researched and included in a Bible story. Most original readers of Scripture knew such background, and Scripture comes alive when its culture is explained. Just be careful not to bog a story down with largely irrelevant details.

There are a few potential problems with the storytelling method. One is the temptation to make the story predictable either by slapping on a "moral of the story" ending or by cramming all stories into a preset mold. Many teachers (and a large percentage of curriculum) succumb to the temptation to stick to familiar stories and familiar approaches, which lends credence to the common perception that the Bible is boring or just a book for little children. Teachers sometimes "apply" the story falsely, then spend the rest of the period emphasizing a lesson that's not really taught in the passage. Other teachers see the Bible story as mainly entertainment, which frees them to stray as far from the biblical record as they want when they tell it or to forget an appropriate level of reverence for God and His Word. But when a story is used well, it can be the most effective method to communicate truth.

Developing your skills as a storyteller and oral communicator should be more basic than honing your skills with visual aids. It's possible to keep children's interested attention without visuals, but the best quality visual aids illustrating mediocre content are a waste of a student's time and rarely keep him interested. Visual aids are important, and they help children remember, but don't expect them to cover for poor storytelling.

Touch, feel, taste, and emotions can be imaginatively described: what wood feels like to a carpenter, the smell of wet trees or wet sheep, the joy of being the member of a crowd Christ fed, the disciples' fear as they locked themselves in the Upper Room in the days between His death and resurrection. You might tell part of the story of Noah's ark from Ham's or Japheth's perspective. You can look at what other passages of Scripture say about a given story. For example, Hebrews 11 gives some details not told in the main tellings of some stories. Or have the children read the story out loud from the Bible, and discuss it as a group. (Don't do this with lengthy passages, or attention will wander.) Get a map and trace Abraham's travels or Christ's preaching tours or Paul's journeys.

Teach with your Bible in your hand or on your lap so that the students remember where the lesson came from. When appropriate, read a verse or two from the Bible as you tell the story. Use a simple outline of the lesson as a bookmark in your Bible; then, if you lose your place in your prepared lesson, you can recover quickly.

Don't try to use the exact wording of the teacher's guide. Learn the structure of the story, but as you tell it, let the children's responses guide your speed, inflections, gestures, and so on. Maintain eye contact. If the boys and girls get bored, involve them by asking questions or having them do some simple action. Remember *why* you're teaching the lesson, and don't get so caught up in the fun details that you forget what the story is about. Don't talk down to them or use undefined words, and don't turn a story into a lecture. Don't finish a story by reviewing the facts: "Jonathan, can you tell me what happened after . . ."

With practice, lesson time can be a highlight for both you and the children, and the rest of the hour can be used for more informal interaction or application exercises that build on the truths of the Bible story.

For Action

1. Look up your favorite story in the Bible, or look at next week's lesson. Read the Scripture passage twice, taking a few notes the second time.

2. Looking only at your notes, tell the story out loud. Then reread the story from Scripture. Were there parts you couldn't remember or that you told wrong? Now tell it again, without your notes if possible.

40

TELLING A BIBLE STORY
Part Two: A Story's Power

*We will not hide them from their children, telling to the
generation to come the praises of the Lord, and His strength and
His wonderful works that He has done.*

(PSALM 78:4)

The story for the week is familiar, and you know that if you start by saying, "Today I'm going to tell you the story of Shadrach, Meshach, and Abednego," Tommy and LaShonda will both raise their hands and say, "Oh! I know it! Let me tell it!" So let's go in a little slower, then let's look at the elements that make a good Bible story.

"The three boys Hananiah, Mishael, and Azariah had known from the time they were little that God could be trusted. They probably had sat on their parents' laps and heard the stories we have been hearing—about Noah, and Moses, and Ruth, and David. They knew how well God had taken care of all of those people. Now the boys were teenagers, and they had just been kidnaped and taken to a strange country. They had probably been scared, but it had helped to remember that God cared about them. And because God had allowed them to stay together in the strange country, they could talk to each other about Him and about their country, Israel. So when they heard they had a choice—they could obey the king and live, or they could obey God and die—the boys, who were now named Shadrach, Meshach, and Abednego, didn't have to think very long at all. This was the hardest test of their lives, but they knew they had to obey God and trust Him."

The paragraph above may not be the way you'd choose to start the story of the three youths. Your personal style will determine much of what works for you and what doesn't. But let's look at a few reasons it could successfully set up this story from Daniel:

- **God's faithfulness is the clear motivator.**
- **Nothing is added to "make things interesting" that might lead kids to remember the fictitious embellishments as facts. All the details are (a) stated in the Bible story or (b) obviously true of young Israelites of that day. Gestures, voice inflections, and visuals can hold interest without your fictionalizing the story.**

- The choice—obey the king and live, or obey God and die—is dramatic, yet it is given before the boys' familiar names are mentioned. This avoids the "I've heard this story before" response you might get if you revealed those names in the first sentence. By coming at the story from a different angle and interesting the listeners before you give away the characters' names, you have greatly increased the chances that students will listen to you.
- It ties this story into the larger picture of biblical history by including the boys with others who came before them. Telling a story within a story is rarely successful when used orally, but the Bible characters mentioned ("the stories we have been hearing about Noah, and Moses, and Ruth, and David") are familiar enough that the mere mention of their names should make the point to many of your students: Yes, God was faithful to all of them.
- It sets the stage for a dramatic story or for a Bible study.

Most adults are not confident of their storytelling ability, and most of us could use more experience. Yet, children love stories. They listen eagerly to a good storyteller, even if the story is familiar. In a day in which children's lives are more and more dominated by the impersonal, mediocre story told by TV or video, the teacher has a wonderful opportunity to hone an older, more effective form: that of the narrator who can make eye contact with his hearers.

A good story is far more than a time filler that children enjoy. Much of the Bible is communicated through stories, and those stories can readily be retold so that children can understand biblical history. Bible stories show application of God's Word in a true situation. Jesus Himself used fictional stories to communicate truths to His listeners. Skits and illustrations can serve the same function today as Jesus' parables did for His audience, though they should never take the place of a lesson from the Bible.

Stories communicate truth in a memorable way. They present Bible people in a way that helps us understand them and their relationship with God. They give boys and girls a model of how to know God, as well as demonstrating His faithfulness. It's much easier to tune out a lecture than a story, because a story involves people at a deeper level.

Before boys and girls can understand difficult truths about God, they can learn to know Him and love Him through stories. Stories capture a child's imagination and his heart, not just his mind. What a child learns to love will interest him more. Too often we forget how truly interesting the Bible is and how powerful are its truths and its images. The creative teacher can do much to keep or rekindle children's interest in what Scripture says by mastering its own primary literary form—the story.

For Action

1. Wait until you are the only person at home, or seek out a quiet place. Get a tape recorder and practice telling a story you know well. Listen to yourself on the tape. What did you do well? Where did you hesitate? What areas of your presentation need work? Now tell the story one more time.

2. Work with this week's Bible lesson. Practice telling it without any props. Practice in front of a mirror, in front of your spouse or kids, or whatever will best help you prepare. After you have done so, figure out what props or visual aids will help you be more effective.

41

EFFECTIVE USE OF VISUAL AIDS

*And Jesus called a little child to Him, set him in the
midst of them, and said, "Assuredly, I say to you, unless
you are converted and become as little children, you will
by no means enter the kingdom of heaven."*

(MATTHEW 18:2–3)

Imagine that you are able to transport a class of third graders who know nothing about the Bible to the actual time and place of Jesus' resurrection. Now you have the best visual aid imaginable. Yet without *words* to explain what happened, who Jesus was, and why His death and resurrection are significant, you still have nothing more than a great illustration. Pictures and other visuals can supplement teaching, but they cannot actually teach truth—that is a job left up to words. But the combination of words and pictures can do much more than either can do alone.

Sometimes it seems teachers choose pictures and props just to have something for kids to look at. Yet a carelessly chosen visual aid is worse than none. I once used curriculum that illustrated all its worksheets with cartoon figures. Since Jesus looked as if He was either on drugs or half asleep, I had to avoid any page that showed Jesus.

Whatever visuals you use, they should supplement your teaching and help the children understand, rather than overpowering the words of Scripture and the lessons they teach. But when words are illustrated with appropriate visual aids, together they draw in the listener, allowing the wandering mind to see as well as hear. Visuals help memory, they increase interest, and they can clarify parts of a story that may be unfamiliar to modern listeners. You probably can easily picture Jesus' disciples wearing robes instead of three-piece suits, because you've seen numerous drawings of people clothed in the garb of the first century. Not all boys and girls can.

Jesus Himself used visual aids effectively. He saw a widow quietly putting the last of her money into the temple treasury. He called His disciples' attention to it and taught them the significance of her action. He beckoned a child to Him and used him as an object lesson. His miracles were visual affirmation of His claims to deity. He walked on the water to His frightened disciples to show them He was truly Master of nature. He healed the blind so that observant Israelites would recognize the validity of His messianic claims (Isaiah 35:5–6). He even raised to life a four-day-old stinking corpse to show that death itself had to submit to Him. His parables and teachings were loaded with visual images: an extravagantly costly pearl, a Samaritan traveler bandaging a nearly dead stranger, a dusty camel making a vain attempt to crawl through a needle's eye.

Because we tend to forget, Scripture throws vivid memorials of biblical truth in our faces, memorials we can see, feel, and even taste. The Lord's Supper reminds us of Christ's broken, bruised body. Baptism says to all the world and the church that this person has changed sides. The temple contained the ark of the covenant, which held its own visual aids—manna and Aaron's rod that budded and the stone tablets with the Ten Commandments in God's own handwriting—lest the people forget.

In our visual age there is definitely a place for carefully chosen props to help a child understand and place himself in Bible times. Drawings of items the children might not be familiar with, maps, or physical objects they can look at or even touch can help make a lesson come alive. You might use a rope dyed red to tell about Rahab; a picture of an altar, the tabernacle, or other items no longer in everyday use to illustrate Old Testament stories; a stuffed lamb or a photograph of a real one when you talk about shepherds; a large nail to illustrate the crucifixion; a homemade scroll to talk about the writing of the Bible.

I like to bring such visuals in a large paper bag and keep them next to me when I teach. If I don't let children peek in the bag ahead of time, they're curious about what's in it. Just reaching for the bag can be enough to bring back wandering minds, and when I pull an object out, I have their full attention.

The heavy use of visual aids can be counterproductive. Too many pictures can stifle a child's ability to visualize a scene, limiting his imagination to what somebody else was able to draw. How many adults still think of Jesus looking the way simplified flannelgraph pictures represented Him? But neglecting to use a few well-chosen visuals limits a child's understanding and gives him a chance to lose focus and start looking at other things or people in the room.

Child Evangelism Fellowship produces many well-illustrated large-format books of good songs for children, as well as illustrated lessons. Children's Bible story books or flash card lessons can offer several good pictures for a given story. Your teacher's guide may have worthwhile suggestions for visual aids, or you may be able to order posters along with your curriculum. Once you have found a good picture, file it for later use—or, if what you have used cannot be filed, write a note for your file telling where it can be found.

And remember, your body language is also a visual aid. Animated gestures or even occasional whispered or shouted words, when appropriate to the story, can draw back wandering attention. If you have done your homework well, you can also slow down to expand on a point when your class's attention is riveted. If you learn the art of good storytelling and good illustration, you may hear many more questions from your attentive class and spend a lot less time disciplining distracted kids.

For Thought

1. For which of the following reasons have you used visuals in your teaching: to help children understand, to help them remember, to keep them interested, to entertain them, to satisfy other teachers and parents, to make up for poor preparation, or to follow the teacher's guide and do everything it tells you to do? Which of the previous reasons are legitimate? Develop a purpose for visual aids.

2. Find two or three visuals that you can use with next week's lesson, and practice using them.

42

TEACHING CHILDREN TO STUDY THE BIBLE

Moreover by them Your servant is warned,
and in keeping them there is great reward.

(Psalm 19:11)

A few years ago I was amazed at how well the fourth- and fifth-grade girls in my small group responded to a devotional based on Isaiah 53. Earlier, the speaker had discussed the Crucifixion, and the day's memory verse was from Isaiah 53, so I had our group read the chapter together and discuss it. I had explained that the chapter was written hundreds of years before Jesus was crucified, so several times girls expressed astonishment at how clearly the verses predicted what later happened to Him. I was delighted by their eagerness and by how well they understood the significance of what they were reading.

It occurred to me after that devotional that popular wisdom may be both underestimating kids' ability to handle the Bible "raw" and doing them a disservice by not adequately preparing them for adult-level Bible study. Consider these characteristics of various age groups:

- Primaries are eager to read.
- Juniors are avid learners.
- Junior-high students face tough questions.
- High schoolers want a challenge.

Meanwhile, adults are often complacent and bored and uninterested in Bible study. The average adult Christian remains at an amazingly low level of Bible knowledge. Could our Sunday school teaching somehow be contributing to the problem of ignorant adults?

I realized when I started thinking through these questions that we usually use three very distinct teaching methods as the child grows from early school years into adulthood: (1) for preschoolers though juniors, the predominant method is the story, though play and workbook learning also have meaningful roles; (2) for junior high and high school students, the emphasis is on "relevance," so lessons are sorted by topic—dating, peer pressure, and so on—usually with more use of discussion, videos, and games than of biblical content; then (3) the young person lands in adult Sunday school, where he or she is somehow expected to know certain theological truths, understand how to study the Bible, and be involved at least to some degree in the biblical disciplines.

Unfortunately, those children who actually do know something about the Bible are in danger of deadly boredom in most church classes, and those who don't pick up the basic facts they should know in childhood enter adulthood without the skills or motivation to learn.

What if it were possible to take advantage of kids' love of learning to instill those principles and facts alongside the stories in a more thorough way than as "the moral of the story"? Is it possible to engage kids in Bible study? And, at the other end of the cycle, is it possible to wake up adults through stories? Must either end be an extreme?

When I started exploring these questions, I spent a semester figuring out how deep junior-age kids could go in occasional structured Bible study. I started with a sword drill (in which they did poorly) to test their familiarity with the Bible and challenge them a bit. Over the next weeks I had them look up the relevant Scripture for most of our lessons. Sometimes we broke into small groups to study specific verses.

One evening we looked at "faith" in Hebrews 11. The previous three lessons had talked about Gideon, who is briefly mentioned in Hebrews 11. As a group we defined faith and listed people and things we might trust, and then the kids looked for names in the chapter. As a name was mentioned, I listed it on the chalkboard and either had the child say how the character showed faith or I told the story briefly myself. So in a short period we had a combination of story, Bible study, and a brief overview of the Old Testament. I asked how the people in Hebrews 11 *showed* their faith, and the kids found the question easy to answer: They obeyed. I hoped the lesson would stick and that the children would see that they can read the Bible for themselves.

Not all of the Bible is story, and boys and girls need to know how to interact with non-narrative texts. I still teach mostly with stories, and I keep focusing on improving my storytelling ability. But I no longer limit myself to that, and I feel free to spend an extra week or two with a topic that a teacher's guide brushes over too quickly. Last year, for example, I spent a couple weeks with the Ten Commandments after the story about how God gave them. Each of the kids had an open Bible, we sat in a circle, and we discussed each commandment: what it meant and why God gave it.

Recently, two young girls I tutor kept asking me questions about heaven. After two weeks of such questions, I brought some Scripture references and a Bible and let them read the text. One girl, who finds reading difficult, read with delight most of a chapter in the somewhat hard words and fine print of the Bible.

Last week a second-grade boy arrived for Sunday school before I did. When I came in, he was reading the Bible silently. After greeting him and chatting with him for a moment, I turned to write something on the board. Behind me, a totally absorbed little boy was exclaiming, "Wow!" and, "Cool!" When I sat down again, he told me in his own words the story he had just read.

How can you help your students start on a lifetime of Bible study?

For Action

1. Read the sample Bible studies in appendix A. Now make notes about some methods that might work with your students.

2. Look at your current series of lessons to see if any of them can be expanded to a second lesson, in order to add a Bible study session for your students.

43

WORKING WITH KIDS WHO BLOW THE CURVE

But solid food belongs to those who are of full age, that is,
those who by reason of use have their senses exercised to
discern both good and evil.

(HEBREWS 5:14)

Bradley knew the answer to practically every question I asked the class. Often he filled in details I hadn't covered when I taught the lesson, making clear that his family was teaching the Bible at home. But his answers weren't just parroted information; they showed that he had thought through what the text meant. He asked perceptive questions, such as, "How did people know what God wanted them to do before the Ten Commandments?"

A challenge in many classes is to bridge the gap between children like Bradley and children like Theresa, the "first-timer" who asks, "What's the New Testament?" Much of the teacher's effort is directed to helping children like Theresa understand unfamiliar vocabulary and helping the average children find 1 Corinthians. Too often that means the boys and girls like Bradley eventually find Sunday school pretty boring. But kids like Bradley—who loves God, is being trained to understand Scripture, and consistently attends church with his family—are the future of the church.

How do we challenge these children and still teach the other boys and girls? How do we keep them interested? The well-taught children, after all, are going to learn Scripture thoroughly from their parents, with or without our help. That is how it should be: Biblically, the main responsibility for teaching Scripture to children falls on the parents. Yet, unfortunately, the very advantage these boys and girls have often turns into a disadvantage in class if only one or two other students are beyond remedial Bible learning. Besides the great risk of boredom, they risk pharisaical pride or self-righteousness because of their greater knowledge. They may become the class showoffs or even the bored ones who misbehave.

A basic principle in helping children avoid spiritual pride is: Avoid giving the idea that certain spiritual actions will win Brownie points with the teacher. There's a fine line between saying, "Amanda, I'm glad you've learned the books of the Bible" and showing off the child as your trophy (and the teacher's pet).

One day Chris, Robert, and Tony, three boys in our club program, stayed after the lesson and expressed interest in receiving Christ as their Savior. (A leader told me afterward that he suspected Robert was just imitating his friends.) Later in the session, Tony pulled another leader aside and asked him to pray for Robert, because he didn't think Robert had really understood the Gospel. With a smile for the new convert's spiritual discernment, the leader came over and told me about the prayer request. He then saw that Tony was looking our way, so he said a little louder, "Yes, Tony, I was just telling Cheryl about your prayer request." I wasn't at all surprised when Tony drew me aside with "another prayer request" a few minutes later and when his attitude the second time was that of a child looking for praise.

Teaching in a fresh way can unearth Bible treasure that is new to both the unchurched student and the more advanced one and is neither boring nor incomprehensible to either. A teacher taught a week's lessons at Bible camp. She focused on giving a broad overview of the Old Testament's storyline, summarizing several consecutive stories each day. The method gave a good introduction for newcomers and also helped children who knew a lot of Bible stories to see how they tied together. Getting students deeply into Scripture allows them to see things they've never seen before.

At some point, "graduating" bored kids into service for the church may be more appropriate than keeping them in a class with their peers when their interest is lagging and their spiritual muscles are atrophying for lack of use. Growing up in a family that had daily devotions, regular church attendance, and a stress on Scripture memory, I was one of those kids. The church "lost" me to adult Sunday school classes for a few years, starting when I was in fourth grade. I lost the peer interaction, but I liked Sunday school again. In later years, I was far happier teaching Sunday school myself than trying to get something out of high school classes that were geared to people with far less Bible background.

And isn't that the biblical pattern, anyway—to learn so that we can worship God, practice what we have learned, and teach others (2 Timothy 2:2; Hebrews 5:12), not so that we can sit in class year after year? I think a thorough, discipleship-centered teaching program could do far more to use even our children in active service than most churches ever consider doing.

For Thought

1. Do you have any students like Bradley in your class? How can you challenge and interest them? How can they be challenged outside the classroom?

2. Make a list of five things Christian third graders can do to serve God. (For example, witnessing at school or visiting in a nursing home with their families or the church.) Can your church include its children and teenagers in any of these?

44

TEACHING CHILDREN TO PRAY

One of His disciples said to Him, "Lord, teach us
to pray, as John also taught his disciples."

(LUKE 11:1)

For years I tried to figure out how a teacher can encourage boys and girls to pray. Over and over, in many different settings teaching children, I asked for a volunteer who wanted to pray. Some child would respond eagerly, and the whole class would bow their heads. Then would come the moment of truth . . . or, usually, the moment of silence. Finally, I would prompt quietly, "Ruth, didn't you want to pray?" No, the child will tell me; she had changed her mind, or she couldn't think of anything to say. Year after year I thought the same thing, *There has to be some way to get kids to pray. But what?*

There is no easy answer to that question, but I have found a good starting point: Be specific about what they should pray about. After a story about Christ's gentleness with Peter, ask, "Who wants to thank God that He is patient with us?" After a lesson on the Great Commission, ask, "Who would like to pray that God would give us courage to tell our friends that we are Christians?" Providing them with a structure helps. When you suggest talking to God and telling Him, "Thank You, God, for . . ." a whole circle of students may pray aloud, with some of them praying several sentences.

Many times the child who volunteers will actually pray about something else. Sometimes timidity will still set in. Last week my volunteer bowed her head, then admitted, "I'm not good at praying."

I told her gently, "You don't have to be good at it. You can just tell God thank You."

So, quietly, she said, "Thank You," and I said, "Amen." Then another child wanted to pray, so I nodded permission. By the way, a teacher's overly lengthy prayers are likely to intimidate or bore children. If you keep your own prayers in class short and conversational, the boys and girls will learn naturally to talk to God.

Teaching the Lord's Prayer is another good way to teach them to pray. In fact, when Jesus' disciples wanted Him to teach *them* to pray, He didn't give them a lesson in prayer but a prayer to pray.

What do boys and girls pray about in their own lives? A few months ago an unusually large number of children requested prayer on our church's prayer sheet, so I kept the sheet to show you their requests. The children range from primary through junior high. I have changed only the names of the people for whom they requested prayer:

- I pray for my family and friends. I pray for my sisters and that I get good grades. I pray that I can go to Science Camp.
- Dear Lord, I want you to give my uncle some more heart. I don't want him to do the things he is doing now.
- Pray that I will be able to put my whole mind into schoolwork for the next couple of weeks.
- Dear God, I thank you for helping my mother and me get up this morning. I'm going to try to give thanks and read the Bible more, God. Bless my brother, because he is doing a lot of bad things in his life. Thank you for helping me not complain.
- Please pray that I will use good judgment and not fall into temptations.
- God, help me, because my friend Rachel died [murdered by her uncle].
- Pray for my daddy to come to church.
- Please pray that I do well in school so I can pass eighth grade and study hard, too. And please pray that I get accepted into Roberto Clemente [High School].
- Dear Lord, thank You for everything You done this week. You blessed my mother and father by them starting to read the Bible and my father to start working on the house. Bless my big brother, Daniel, so that he gets an apartment. And bless my other brother, Martin, who is in jail. And I hope my mother gets this job.
- Lord, I want to pray for my grandmother who is very sick, but I know you are going to heal her very well. I also want to pray for my family.

Cheri Fuller explains, "We adults tend to see obstacles and analyze complications until our problems begin to look like a mountain. We ask, *How can God do anything?* Kids, on the other hand, have a wonderfully simple trust. They believe God is bigger than the mountain, that He can move anything and provide anything."[1]

A teacher must not give the impression that prayer is like a wish list given to Santa Claus. Prayer needs to focus on who God is, not just on what He can do for us. And children need to understand that praying is not a spiritual work that somehow earns points with God. As far as I can see in Scripture, He never promises to answer the prayers of unbelievers (though He may choose to do so), and He never promises to answer a prayer that is outside His will. But God loves children, and I believe He enjoys hearing them learn to pray to Him while they are young.

Jesus said, "Let the little children come to me, and do not hinder them, for the kingdom of heaven belongs to such as these" (Matthew 19:14 NIV). Often we find ourselves re-translating that to suggest that He said, "Let the children listen to somebody talking about Me." No, He wants them to come *to Him*. Sometimes we need to provide the opportunity and quietly move out of the way.

Note
1. Cheri Fuller, *When Children Pray: How God Uses the Prayers of a Child* (Sisters, Ore.: Multnomah, 1998), 32.

For Action

1. List three "prayer starter" sentences or phrases you can use in your class.

2. Look at your lesson for next week. How can you encourage children to respond in prayer to God? Make a note of one or two ways in your lesson notes.

45

TEACHING MEMORIZATION

*Your word I have hidden in my heart, that I might
not sin against You!*

(PSALM 119:11)

When I was a child, Scripture memorization was an important part of children's Sunday school classes, and Christian parents encouraged their children to memorize additional verses—even whole chapters—at home. For several years I was enrolled in Bible Memory Association, an organization that provided a structure for kids (and adults) to learn several verses a week for a few months out of each year. Dozens of those verses still come to mind readily.

Today, though, Scripture memorization has gotten a bad rap, even in some Sunday school curricula. Books about teaching tell stories of boys and girls who felt they could never measure up because they weren't good at learning verses. They tell of others who felt spiritually superior because they knew dozens of verses by heart—without putting any of them into practice. But Scripture memory is not the problem; the problem is that verses are taught and memorized by imperfect, sinful people.

Our culture is shying away from memorization in public school and in the church. But whatever culture decides is a good idea or a bad idea, remember that *God* is the one who said it's good to memorize Scripture.

Some Christian educators have legitimate concerns about Scripture memory. Many say that rote learning (learning facts or words without necessarily understanding the meaning) is a lower level of learning. Clearly it is important to help children understand what they are memorizing, but must one fully understand the multiplication table to memorize it or find it useful? Most children who learn the books of the Bible do so before they have the slightest idea what "Lamentations" means. But then, most kids also learn the alphabet before they know how to read. Memorizing the books of the Bible doesn't make one a good Christian, but it makes Bible study easier and helps students develop a structure for understanding the Bible.

Yes, rote learning is a lower level of learning, and we shouldn't stop there. But don't avoid teaching memorization for fear that it's useless.

Should a teacher teach a verse every week? Should other activities be bumped aside for Scripture memory? It depends, among other things, on how much time you have. I heard one suggestion that seems wise: It's better to teach one verse a month that students actually learn than to teach a verse each week that children can recite for a few minutes but that they never really learn. When I taught the Ten Commandments, I spent several weeks teaching the verse that summarized them in Jesus' words (Mark 12:30). Last year, for a series of lessons about the church, the class kept coming back to Matthew 16:18, Jesus' promise to build His church no matter what hell tried to do.

What version of the Bible should you use? The King James or something else? The question is a tricky one, because there are two clear sides, and both feel very strongly. Some will say that you should only use the King James, and some will say you should use anything but the King James. You may be curious to know which side I'm most willing to offend!

I would say don't use a paraphrase (such as *The Living Bible* or *The Message*) rather than a translation, and don't use a children's version. Children will outgrow "children's Bibles," and most families won't be using them anyway. Beyond those two criteria, consider what most adults in your church use. If they use the King James, lobbying for the NIV or some other version will cause needless offense—use the King James (or the *New King James* if that is acceptable to parents and church leadership). Likewise, if most adults use the *New American Standard Version* or the *New International Version* or the *New Living Translation,* using the KJV will likely confuse both kids and their parents.

Don't be afraid of using a Bible that has some words children won't understand—explaining the meaning is part of teaching the verse. If you have to choose between biblical accuracy and a version that's easily understood, go with accuracy and explain.

But how can a teacher even teach Bible memory today? Below are a few creative ways to have the boys and girls read the verse several times or repeat it several times. Do make sure your methods don't trivialize Scripture or turn memorization into a contest for spiritual credit with God or the teacher.

1. Have children copy the verse and illustrate it. As they draw, ask one child if he can say (or read) the verse for you. Then ask another to tell you what the verse means.

2. Give children small pieces of paper and very sharp pencils. Challenge them to see who can write the verse in the smallest space. (Most students will end up writing it several times in the attempt.)

3. Ask for volunteers to go with another leader and make up a tune for the verse, while you lead the rest of the class in a different activity. Then have the volunteers teach the verse to their tune.

4. Have the boys and girls look up the verse in their Bibles, and let several take turns reading it aloud. Then see who can say it without looking. Between kids' saying the verse, intersperse questions about the meaning. That makes sure they understand, and it also helps ensure that they are actually learning the verse, not just repeating the same sentence another child just finished saying.

For other ideas, look in your teacher's guide or pick up a book on teaching memory verses from the Christian education section of your Christian bookstore.

For Action

1. Look to see what your teacher's guide suggests as this week's memory verse. Does it fit? If no verse is provided, or if the suggested verse does not fit, see if you can find a verse in the passage you're teaching or a good verse on the same topic elsewhere.

2. Do you think it would be helpful to teach the verse you have chosen? If so, look in the list above or in another resource and choose a method for teaching it. Also prepare copies of the verse that your students can take home.

46

EXPLAINING THE GOSPEL
Part One: The Importance of the Right Words

All Scripture is given by inspiration of God, and is profitable for doctrine, for reproof, for correction, for instruction in righteousness, that the man of God may be complete, thoroughly equipped for every good work.

(2 TIMOTHY 3:16–17)

For some reason, "ask Jesus into your heart" has become one of the most popular ways to describe salvation when talking to children. I personally don't use that phrase because it's vague and it's not found in Scripture. But whatever wording you use when talking about salvation, the Gospel needs to be explained clearly. For example, you could say:

> The Bible says that God is holy. That means God is perfect. He has never done anything wrong. You and I have done wrong—sinned—and we can never be good enough to have our sins overlooked by God. Sin is anything you and I do that displeases Him, like . . . [give an example or two appropriate to the age of your children]. Because God loves us very much, even though we have sinned, He sent His Son, Jesus, to earth. Jesus lived a perfect life. Then He died on the cross to pay for our sins, and then He came back to life. [If you have not done so previously in the hour, go into a little more detail about Christ's death.] If you ask Him to forgive your sins, He will. [Read at least one Scripture verse about salvation so that a child who is not ready or is too shy to respond to the invitation can still hear what the Bible says.] If you have never asked Jesus to forgive your sins and be your Savior, and you want to do that today, you can stay in the circle after the others go to small groups, and I'll show you more about what the Bible says.

One day I was explaining Romans 6:23, which talks about the gift of God, eternal life. I asked the class, "What do you do to earn your Christmas presents?"

"Be good" was the immediate answer. I tried to challenge the answer: If you are not good, does that mean no Christmas? To my surprise, just about every child in the room was fully convinced he or she *earned* Christmas presents by good behavior. That has huge ramifications on our teaching that salvation is wholly a gift of God's grace!

Child Evangelism Fellowship uses an acrostic that has helped me remember the elements of the Gospel:

G—God is holy and just, and He loves you and me
O—Only perfect, sinless Son of God [Jesus]
S—Sin—you and I [include yourself] have sinned
P—Precious blood of Jesus shed for our sin
E—Ever living [resurrected], coming Savior
L—Let Him in

Look at the following explanations of the Gospel, and see whether they are clear invitations to salvation:

1. Give your life to God. [But does salvation mean giving something to God, or accepting His gift to us?]
2. You need to be saved. [Saved from what? Explain this.]
3. Jesus died so that you can go to heaven to be with God. [Where are sin and salvation in this?]

We're so used to the lingo that we don't even notice when it *replaces* the Gospel. The Gospel does not require a vague prayer saying something about Jesus. The Gospel is *specific* truth about Christ that must be accepted by faith: His death, burial, and resurrection for our sins. Generalized Jesus talk cannot substitute for the Gospel.

Children are fascinated by heaven, and descriptions of hell scare them. Quite often, teachers take advantage of those truths to get a response. Yet when we encourage a child's desire to "go to heaven when you die," we have given an incomplete picture of salvation. The child tantalized to salvation by visions of heaven is unlikely to picture heaven as a place to worship God and get to know Jesus better. He imagines a beautiful place where he'll never be sick and never be spanked. Sure, he wants to go there! On the other hand, hell sounds extremely unpleasant—definitely a place to avoid. Hey, if all it takes to get a ticket to the better place is saying a prayer, why not?

Childhood longing for heaven often sets the stage for a lifelong love affair with Jesus, but it shouldn't be presented as the primary motivation in presentations of the Gospel. Such a presentation avoids the real issues involved: God's holiness, man's separation from God, Christ's provision through the Cross of a way of forgiveness, and acceptance of the Gospel through faith. It's only indirectly true that Jesus died so that we can go to heaven. And it's untrue if we picture heaven as a lovely vacation spot rather than as a place to worship and serve God without earthly hindrances. Heaven and hell must be linked with the most significant part of what they are: intimacy with God or eternal separation from Him based on His righteous punishment of sin.

It's also untrue that Jesus died for us because we were so valuable He somehow couldn't resist doing so. He died because of His love, not our lovableness. He also didn't die to *help us* get to heaven; He died because it was the only way we could approach God. I find that no matter how many times I go over the Gospel, some children keep going back to the idea that we are saved by our good works. I keep returning to Scripture, especially Ephesians 2:8–9.

For Thought

1. How have you explained salvation to children in the past? Was it clear? biblical?

2. Do you think "ask Jesus to come into your heart" is a good way to present the Gospel? Why or why not?

47

EXPLAINING THE GOSPEL
Part Two: The Process

*For I am not ashamed of the gospel of Christ, for it is
the power of God to salvation for everyone who
believes, for the Jew first and also for the Greek.*

(ROMANS 1:16)

*For the message of the cross is foolishness to those who
are perishing, but to us who are being saved it is the
power of God.*

(1 CORINTHIANS 1:18)

Two sisters in my cabin at camp responded to an invitation given by the leader, who had emphasized hell. I went with my students to counsel them. As I asked both in turn, "Why did you raise your hand just now?" and, "What would you like Jesus to do for you?" it became clear that both were responding out of fear of hell. They sensed their need for forgiveness but had no sense of their inability to rescue themselves from their own sins. They were only vaguely familiar with Jesus' death on the cross, and neither knew much about the Bible. I could have told them, "Repeat this prayer after me," and counted it as two salvation decisions, but I was quite sure they did not yet understand. They would have been merely saying words. And nowhere does the Bible suggest that people are saved by saying certain words.

Instead, I gave both girls a brief summary of the Bible's salvation history: Creation, the Fall, the Law, people's inability to keep the Law, Christ's coming, His death and resurrection, His offer of salvation. I emphasized to them that Christ's offer of salvation was completely free; we can't earn it or deserve it. I told them they could talk to me anytime in the week if they had questions, then I prayed briefly and dismissed them.

Did I miss a golden opportunity to win those girls to the Lord, or did I avoid picking green fruit? I believe it was the latter. Later that week, the younger child prayed with me to receive Christ, her older sister expressed excitement that she had learned a lot about God, and I gave both girls Bibles. Although both live some distance from me and I have not seen them since, I still correspond with them.

Pushing children to "say a prayer" when they do not understand is treating prayer as a magical rite that mysteriously saves, and it's showing lack of faith in the Holy Spirit's ability to continue watering a seed you have planted. Discernment can avoid leading a child to false assurance of salvation. What if the child really does understand or understands later? Salvation comes through faith, not through a particular formula, and we can safely allow the Holy Spirit to work in such cases. A human teacher doesn't even have to be present.

But when you do have the chance to present the Gospel to a class, how can you teach it? First, ahead of time, *memorize a few verses* (and their references) so that you can readily show what the Bible says about salvation. Here are several references to look up and consider using: John 3:16; Acts 16:31; 20:28b; Romans 3:23; 5:8–9; 6:23; Ephesians 1:7; 2:8–9; Colossians 1:14; Hebrews 9:22; 1 Peter 3:15; Revelation 1:5. Notice that, with any of these, you must be able to define terms. For instance, Acts 16:31: What does it mean to *believe?* And *what* do we believe about Jesus? What does it mean to *be saved?* What are we saved *from?*

As you explain the Gospel, *help your students to understand sin by giving specific examples* boys and girls can identify with. "Sin is anything we do that makes God unhappy, like being so mad at someone that you don't care if the other person gets hurt, as long as you get what you want."

By the way, try to avoid suggesting sins they may not have thought of. A story in a children's Sunday school paper had a child's friend buying Liquid Paper. He told the child that his mother thought it was for school, but that actually sniffing it made him feel good. Also be sure not to limit your discussion of sin in such a way that children think that only *some* people sin, that only adults sin, or that Christians never sin. My brother Ed told me, "Many times I have gotten a group of children to agree that we are *all* sinners and have done wrong, but when I pointed to one child and asked him if he had ever done anything wrong, to my amazement he shook his head and replied that he had not. This has happened a number of times. It's easy to agree that we are all sinners without making it personal."

Focus on the Cross. Children need to know that we can approach God only through Jesus. I accepted the Lord as my Savior when I was four years old, so I'm well aware that young children can understand their need for salvation. The most rambunctious class is usually quiet when I talk about the Cross. In such settings Satan flees, and the Holy Spirit works. Also, boys and girls have not turned the horrors and the joys of the Cross into mere religious truisms. They feel its weight. They don't have the adult need to feel self-sufficient, so they more readily recognize their need of God. And Jesus calls them to come to Him.

When you invite children to talk to you about salvation, be sure you *don't indicate that the action you suggest* (raising a hand, for example) *is what saves them.* We aren't saved by raising a hand, but we can show a teacher we want to be saved by doing so.

In the next chapter we'll look at how you can lead a child to Christ if one of your students responds to the invitation.

For Action

1. Choose two or three salvation verses from the list above. Be sure you can define them well, and memorize them. Mark them in your Bible.

2. Pretend you are teaching your class. Out loud, explain the Gospel completely and in words your students will understand.

PART 7

APPLYING THE LESSON: BEYOND THE CLASSROOM

I worry about how we will train children to act on their Christian beliefs if they view the narratives of the faith as simply more information that does not really affect their lives.

—MARVA J. DAWN,
Is It a Lost Cause? Having the Heart of God for the Church's Children (Grand Rapids: Eerdmans, 1997), 183.

48

LEADING A CHILD TO CHRIST

There will be more joy in heaven over one sinner
who repents than over ninety-nine just persons
who need no repentance.

(LUKE 15:7)

Y ears ago I learned that the key to counseling children for salvation is asking good questions.[1] Salvation is not a formula, but good questions can help a child understand and articulate his decision. Children respond to an invitation for numerous reasons: A child may misunderstand what the invitation is for. He may already be saved but feel guilty about some recent sin that he wants to confess. He may even believe that committing sin means he is no longer saved. A child may just want someone to talk with him. He may want to go to heaven but have no awareness that he is a sinner who needs to be forgiven. He may respond because a friend raised his hand. Or when you thought he was raising his hand, he may have just been scratching an itch. Good questions narrow down to the real reason a student responded. Let's look at several good questions, in the order in which you could ask them.

- **Why did you want to talk to me today?**
- **What do you want Jesus to do for you?**

If the child says he wants to ask Jesus to forgive his sins, ask:

- **Have you ever done this before?**

If he says he has done so previously, ask him to tell you about that time. If it seems quite clear he is already saved, go over Christ's promise never to leave him (Hebrews 13:5) and ask if he wants to pray and thank Jesus for that promise. Sometimes the child prayed a "salvation prayer" at an earlier date, but questioning him will reveal that he really didn't know what was going on when he did so. If you aren't sure whether he was truly saved previously, you can still go over verses of assurance, say that if he has trusted Christ to forgive him for his sins, then Christ has done so, and ask if he'd like to talk to God. I don't suggest a "salvation prayer" at such a point—I'd rather turn the student to Scripture and let it reassure or convict rather than just suggest further prayers, as though eventually one will probably stick.

If the child has never asked Jesus to be his Savior, it's time to move to some other questions to test his understanding:

- Have you ever done anything that makes Jesus unhappy?
- What did Jesus do to take care of your sins?
- What did Jesus promise to do if you ask Him to forgive your sins?

Now, if not before, it is important to sit down and actually look at Scripture with the child. Depending on his level of understanding, you may need to do quite a thorough overview of what the Bible says. If the child already understands that he is a sinner and that Jesus died for him, stick to one or two verses that contain the Gospel. I turn to the verse and have the child read it, asking him to explain it to me or explaining it to him. (Several possible verses were listed in the previous chapter.)

Once I am sure the child understands, I ask him two more questions, one of them a repeated question:

- What would you like Jesus to do for you?
- What would you like to say to Jesus?

The second question sets the groundwork for actually praying. If his answer is vague ("I want to say I'm sorry"), you can prompt him with further questions. At this point, if he does not really understand, he may be trying to get the "right" words to make you happy, so be careful in your questioning. Once you are quite sure the child understands and knows what he wants to say, ask, "Are you ready to tell Jesus right now what you just told me?"

I have found it's much better to let boys and girls pray in their own words—out loud, if they are willing. That makes the words their own, and it gives the teacher a chance to see their level of understanding. Most of the time children will add to the points they've agreed they want to tell Jesus. They will go on to thank Him for other things or express delight in who He is and what He did for them. If only for my own joy in eavesdropping on such joyful prayers, I do my best to avoid saying a prayer for the child to repeat after me. When the child says his own prayer, the teacher can use his own words in follow-up: "Did you mean it when you said, 'Jesus, I really want You to forgive me'? What do you think Jesus did when you asked Him to forgive you?"

One caution: Don't tell a child he is now saved. Leave confirmation of that to Scripture and to the Holy Spirit. (You don't know that he is saved, and you don't want to give false assurance.) Instead, ask him what he just told Jesus and what Jesus promised to do for him. Then, if you have time, spend a few minutes looking at follow-up Scriptures such as Hebrews 13:5 and 1 John 1:9. Encourage the child by telling him that he can learn more about God by reading the Bible. This would be a good time to give a few tips, such as what chapters to read. You can also encourage him to tell other people about Jesus, to pray, and to attend church.

Give him a follow-up leaflet or a piece of paper on which you have written out the salvation verse(s) you used (not just the reference) and a few other verses. Then encourage him to tell another leader what he has just done. That ensures that the first person he tells will be someone who will treat his new birth as good news. But don't announce his decision in front of the class, or other children may want to "accept Christ" just to please you.

Note

1. Many of the questions in this chapter are based on questions I learned in Child Evangelism Fellowship training.

For Thought

1. What would be the purpose for each of the sample questions listed in this chapter? (Review each one to be sure you understand.)

2. How can you follow up a child who has asked Jesus to forgive his sins?

49

PRAYING FOR YOUR STUDENTS

*And this I pray, that your love may abound still more
and more in knowledge and all discernment, that you
may approve the things that are excellent, that you may
be sincere and without offense till the day of Christ,
being filled with the fruits of righteousness which are by
Jesus Christ, to the glory and praise of God.*

(PHILIPPIANS 1:9–11)

Several years ago a good friend was teaching thirteen-year-old Holly. Holly's father was an elder in the church, but he wasn't very involved in the life of his family. And neither of Holly's parents apparently knew what my friend knew—that one of Holly's most significant goals for eighth grade was to lose her virginity.

One week Holly came to Sunday school excited. She whispered to her friends that she was going to an important party on Friday and that *that* could be the night (which should point out, by the way, the importance of paying attention to what your kids talk about when they don't think you're listening).

My friend, heartsick, sought out her fellow teacher, who also knew the situation. The two of them prayed with earnest tears that God would intervene in this child's plan. The following week Holly came to church in a full-leg cast because she had broken her leg Thursday night. My friend could hardly hold back her grin at God's creative answer to their prayer.

What you teach in the classroom won't stick beyond Sunday morning (or Tuesday night, or whenever you teach) if your involvement in the class is limited to seeing the boys and girls for an hour a week and spending a few quick, unreflective minutes in preparation beforehand. Besides occasionally contacting the children outside of class and being sure to spend adequate time preparing your lesson, a good way to affect your students' lives is to pray for them. As you pray, God will connect your heart to them, even softening you toward the boys and girls you find it hard to like. As you pray, you will want to find out more about them and to discover what their needs are. When you see them in class, you will remember needs they mention and will pray for them later.

When fourth graders tell their deepest needs, many of the problems will wound your heart. "I haven't seen my dad for two years, and I'm supposed to see him this weekend, but he's in the hospital." "My parents are talking about divorce." "My best friend got arrested because he brought a knife to school." "My uncle may get out of jail next week." "My family maybe gonna move, and I hope we don't." "Both of my grandmas just died." Listen to their needs, and intercede for them to God.

Many of the New Testament letters give good models of how to pray for your students. See the verses from Philippians at the head of this chapter. Look up Colossians 1:9–10; 2 Thessalonians 1:11–12; Hebrews 13:20–21; and 3 John 2. It encourages me to know that, the night before Jesus' crucifixion, He prayed for me and for my students. John records His prayer like this: "I do not pray for these alone, but also for those who will believe in Me through their word; that they all may be one, as You, Father, are in Me, and I in You; that they also may be one in Us, that the world may believe that You sent Me" (John 17:20–21).

As you pray for your children, find out where they stand with God. Which of them are believers, and which are not? Which aren't sure? Which ones say they are but show no evidence? Which ones are being distracted by the appeal of sin or by heartaches too big for a child?

Some teachers like to use photographs of each child as a reminder to pray. I have photos of several at-risk boys on my wall at work and more photos of some of my favorite children on my refrigerator at home. Other teachers post lists of names or even fill out forms with specific facts about each child in their class. Find a method that works for you and talk to God about your children before you talk to them about God.

For Action

1. Write down a list of all your regular students. Beside each name, write at least one need that student has. Can't think of one? Try to speak to that child in private next week and ask, "What would you like me to pray about?"

2. Write down the names of your irregular students or boys and girls who have not attended recently. If you have phone numbers, call each one, tell him you hope to see him in class next week, and ask what you can pray about before then. If you have an address but no phone number, send a post card saying you prayed for the child today and you miss him.

50

"FOLLOW ME AS I FOLLOW CHRIST"

Remember those who rule over you, who have spoken the word of God to you, whose faith follow, considering the outcome of their conduct.

(HEBREWS 13:7)

Several years ago, after an Arizona thunderstorm, I walked past a new office complex that had young trees planted in front. I felt some sadness when I saw more than a half dozen of the trees bent over, almost touching the ground. Glancing at one sapling, I noticed that its trunk was still strong and supple. The post that had once supported it, however, had broken in the storm, and the weight of that broken stick was causing a healthy young tree to bend in half. I looked further, and the same proved to be true of the whole row of trees.

In a sense, adults are the stakes young lives are tied to. Loving, godly parents and teachers encourage boys and girls toward growth and fruitfulness. In contrast, abusive, neglectful, or immoral adults can warp children's lives.

Does it bother you to think how devastated and disillusioned the children you teach would be if they saw you making sinful choices? Paul said numerous times and in various ways, "Follow me as I follow Christ." Christ Himself said over and over, "Follow Me." But what if you *don't* follow Christ? What happens to the kids following you?

Children admire their teachers, and they have in mind what standards to expect from them. That they can answer our endless story questions about what Johnny should do in a particular setting shows that—at least in a multiple-choice quiz—they can figure out the "Christian" response. But what do they say and do when we aren't around?

Several years ago two girls came to me with some concern showing on their faces. They had found the definition for a sexual term written in the back of my teenage assistant's Bible. If that had been the end of the story, the obvious application would be that we need to act like Christians so that the kids we teach won't be disappointed. Actually, the truth is scarier than that.

Kids do know what leaders should act like, but they won't necessarily be traumatized if we don't act that way. Later in the day, I heard a boy ask one of the girls, "What were you laughing at earlier?" She told him about the definition, and she told him what she hadn't told me—the exact wording, which described what teenagers could get away with behind their parents' backs. And she giggled. In other words, the girls knew what to say to me, but with other kids they could report an authority figure's rebellion as humorous.

A friend told me about a similar encounter. Some teenagers had eavesdropped on her, misinterpreted something she said, then gleefully reported their misinformation to the rest of the youth group. And the youth group treated their Sunday school teacher like a hero . . . because they thought she was having sex with her boyfriend.

Children and young people hear from the media and people they respect that chastity is an unrealistic and unnecessary goal, that most young people drink alcohol before they're of legal age, that teens can figure out their own moral choices by themselves, and that pornography is a normal interest for young boys (and even girls). The statistics are omnipresent in their insistence that immorality is "normal" for teenagers. The church's own legacy has been tarnished by scandals. As much as your students may know the right answers in class, they may think those are "church" answers that don't affect the rest of the week—and they may assume the same is true in your life.

Please, for the sake of Christ, let them see your life. Follow Christ closely that, as your students see your life and follow you, they'll also learn to follow Him. But rely on the Holy Spirit, not your own personal goodness. As James Montgomery Boice says, unbelievers need "not so much the evidence of righteousness in us, which they can copy by their own fleshly efforts, as living demonstrations of God's grace, which they need but cannot copy."[1]

Note

1. James Montgomery Boice, "On My Mind: Repenting Always," *Modern Reformation* 8, no. 2 (March/April 1999): 40.

For Evaluation

1. Before God, examine your life. Is there an area that could act as a "broken stake" for the children you teach?

2. What is your attitude toward the authority God has placed over you (Scripture, supervisors, government, police, church elders, etc.)? Are there areas in which your attitude has said, "Yeah, follow me, but don't worry about obeying *them*"?

51

WORKING WITH YOUR STUDENTS' PARENTS

[I am] greatly desiring to see you, being mindful of your tears, that I may be filled with joy, when I call to remembrance the genuine faith that is in you, which dwelt first in your grandmother Lois and your mother Eunice, and I am persuaded is in you also.

(2 TIMOTHY 1:4–5)

A teacher mentioned to a group of teachers that he had a problem with one of his students, who was not obeying. Another teacher gave advice right away: "Talk to her mother." I suggested that a better first step would be to take the child aside and talk to her. The teacher could explain the problem, reiterate his love for the child, and underscore the need for obedience. He could tell her that he might need to talk to her mother but that he wanted to first give her another chance on her own.

The combination of warning the child that a parent could be involved soon, the fact that the teacher has respected him enough to allow him a chance to avoid that step, and the personal attention shown often works wonders. Many children are terrified of a teacher's bad report to a parent, so telling Mom or Dad may be more drastic than necessary for minor uncharacteristic misbehavior. But when the child continues to misbehave with no obvious effort at improvement, it's time to prove you weren't bluffing.

Some parents want to know anytime their child is misbehaving, and some would rather not hear anything. Some parents expect their child to obey them, and the child may take advantage of being under another adult's care by seeing if he can disobey someone else. And some boys and girls disobey their teachers because their parents never really expect them to obey at home and the children haven't yet realized their teachers *do*. Some children live with grandparents, foster parents, or in some other living situation. A variety of students brings a variety of parental expectations to teachers. The standing rule for parental interaction is to back up the parents' authority by speaking respectfully of the parent to the child and respecting the parents' God-given position in the child's life when you talk to the parent.

Some mothers and fathers will back up your discipline, some may undermine it, and some won't care—but do back up *their* discipline, even if you don't agree with every detail. The obvious exception—suspected child abuse—is a subject that requires expertise I don't have. If you face that situation, talk to your supervisor in the program. Be aware that the supervisor may then be required legally to report it. You, as a volunteer, probably are not, but state laws vary.

Ideally, interaction with moms and dads should go deeper than issues of misbehavior. Unfortunately, you probably don't have time to get to know the entire families of each of your students, but making some effort toward that ideal will help your teaching. It will bring you into partnership and, hopefully, mutual respect with the parents. Listen to their concerns about the class or their tips about interacting with their children, and see them as potentially your biggest allies.

Mark DeVries writes:

Sunday school and youth group have become a substitute for religious training in the home. Interestingly enough, the Sunday-school movement itself began as an outreach to unchurched poor children. Its founders never intended for it to take over the role of Christian parents.[1]

Deuteronomy 6:7 was talking to Israelite parents, and by extension to all parents who are believers, when it said, "You shall teach them [the truths you know about God] diligently to your children, and shall talk of them when you sit in your house, when you walk by the way, when you lie down, and when you rise up."

Parents may occasionally approach you as though you were the "paid professional," solely responsible for the religious education of their children. Unless they are unbelievers, try gently to put the primary responsibility back in their hands, where it belongs. You might suggest some good books or other resources to them, or tell your pastor that you see a need for families to be taught how to teach their children. If the parents are not believers, they may be open to letting you come alongside and teach them about Christ.

Today's parents, even lifelong Christians, are largely unable to teach their children in any meaningful way, and they are often too immersed in our culture to recognize its dangers. Yet mothers and fathers, who interact with their children every day, can challenge boys and girls more specifically and hold them more accountable.

In Bible accounts, families participated in worship together, and parents taught their sons and daughters at home what they did not yet understand. Jewish children also received formal synagogue education. The system was based on the sensed need to thoroughly train boys and girls, giving them the best possible preparation for God-fearing adulthood. Today, churches rarely treat children as members of families, and we rarely keep families together. Mostly, children are put in the care of largely untrained lay people who are given as much authority as highly trained professionals.

Last year I started the Sunday school year by sending a letter home to all the parents. In it I introduced myself briefly, gave an overview of the semester's lessons, told the Scripture passage we would be emphasizing and memorizing, explained my desire to come alongside them supporting their teaching of their children, and gave my home phone number. The next week, one or two parents expressed appreciation that I had made an effort to work in the same direction with them, which was what I had in mind.

Note

1. Mark DeVries, *Family-Based Youth Ministry* (Downers Grove, Ill.: InterVarsity, 1994), 165.

For Action

1. Write a letter to your students' parents telling them a little about what you are teaching in the class and inviting them to get to know you.

2. Write down a plan for intentionally working with the parents of your students.

52

CONNECTING CHILDREN TO THE CHURCH

Gather the people together, men and women and little ones . . . that they may hear and that they may learn to fear the Lord your God and carefully observe all the words of this law.

(DEUTERONOMY 31:12)

How would it change your life if you believed that nobody needs you—not your spouse, your children, your friends, your coworkers? Some people might miss you if you were dead, but what if not one person actually needs what you bring to a relationship or a task? That's the situation in which most of today's children and teenagers find themselves. They are expendable, and too often they believe they and adults are only in each other's way.

The church is supposed to be different. The church is a community comprising all ages, nationalities, income categories, and levels of intelligence. We're asking too little of our children, and giving them too little in return, when we see them only as people who will *someday* be part of the church. Believing children are *already* part of the body of Christ. Unbelieving children are integral parts of their families and thus are important parts of the church community. Even boys and girls can learn the Twenty-third Psalm, the Lord's Prayer, and the doxology. They can be involved in the worship service, encourage the pastor, pray for fellow believers, and minister to each other and the rest of the body.

It is interesting to observe a group of children who have a purpose for what they are doing, whether they are participating in gymnastics, singing in a youth choir, or playing softball. When they consider themselves a necessary part of the action, they are focused, involved, and interested. Which child is more likely to misbehave: the "useless" child on the bench or the one whose team is counting on him?

One week when I was a camp counselor, I decided to acquaint the girls in my cabin with the truths behind "Great Is Thy Faithfulness," a song they probably all knew. I had looked up Scripture verses beforehand, and I brought a visualized version of the song. Each day after discussing the words to one stanza and looking up related verses as a group, we sang the song together. On the day the stanza talked about the wonders of God's creation, we had devotions outside.

It was clear in the first session or two that the girls found my devotions less than exciting. Singing a hymn as a group seemed to strike them as uncool. Nevertheless I persevered, wanting them to grasp the meaning of God's faithfulness and wanting them to understand the song more fully the next time they sang it in church. By the end of the week, the girls were taking part in the discussions more enthusiastically, and they were singing the song as though they meant it.

Often churches do everything they can to separate children from adults, fearing that the kids will be bored if they are in a setting where they don't understand everything—and also, I suspect, trying to give the parents a break from dealing with them. But adults need to see children's unashamed love and eager faith, and children need the adults' guidance—not just the guidance of "professional" teachers but also of their own parents and other adults in the church, including the pastor. When their only contact with adults in the church is with professionals or volunteers, they may think leaders are all paid to deal with them, suspecting that no one would do so for free.

During Old Testament assemblies, the Law was sometimes read for hours. Yet those occasions did not necessarily exclude children. Nehemiah 8 tells of one such audience that consisted of "men and women and all who were able to understand" (vv. 2–3). Though this gathering lasted all morning, everyone listened attentively as the leaders read and explained Scripture. Joel 2:16 even includes "the children and nursing babes" in a sacred assembly. Joshua 8:35 says Joshua read all of Moses' law in front of the whole community, including the "little ones," and Deuteronomy 29:10–13 describes the whole community—again including the "little ones"—gathering to "enter into covenant with the Lord your God, and into His oath, which the Lord your God makes with you today."

Marva Dawn says,

> I believe it is a sacred duty (and also a great delight) for all the members of the congregation to affirm our community's youth, to greet them warmly and welcome their participation in all our activities, to ask about what is important to them and to encourage them, to be a small part of forming them into godly young people.[1]

Boys and girls who are in the larger community can learn from believers of all ages, including senior saints and older children. The older kids, in turn, can learn by helping younger ones and being accountable as role models to them. Even in a carefully monitored church setting, children often learn more bad than good from peers. To the degree that a larger number of adults are involved in their lives and observing their behavior, that problem is lessened. When children don't give back to the community and aren't expected to, they learn unconsciously that they aren't needed, and they develop a consumer mentality. Is that part of the reason churches have a hard time recruiting volunteers from those who are considered old enough to work in the church?

Believing boys and girls are beginners who need instruction, but they are also members of today's church, not just tomorrow's. As Paul said to Timothy, so I want to say to the children I teach: "Don't let anyone look down on you because you are young, but set an example for the believers in speech, in life, in love, in faith and in purity" (1 Timothy 4:12 NIV).

Note

1. Marva J. Dawn, *Is It a Lost Cause? Having the Heart of God for the Church's Children* (Grand Rapids: Eerdmans, 1997), 58.

For Thought

1. List two ways you can help make the children you teach an integral part of the church community.

2. List two suggestions you can make to church leadership about making the boys and girls of the church more visibly part of the community. (Examples: listing children's names with their parents in the church directory, including examples of children in the pastor's sermon illustrations.)

AFTERWORD: OUR GREAT HOPE

At that time you were without Christ, being aliens from the commonwealth of Israel and strangers from the covenants of promise, having no hope and without God in the world.

(EPHESIANS 2:12)

For I know the thoughts that I think toward you, says the Lord, thoughts of peace and not of evil, to give you a future and a hope.

(JEREMIAH 29:11)

A friend and former roommate, Yvette Metzger, reported the saddest thing about an internship working with junior high and high school students: the hopelessness that many of them had in meeting life. Youth is supposed to be a time for dreams, yet today adolescence takes a heavy toll. The bad-news media, gloomy music, and the realities of teenage culture conspire to encourage despondency. Suicide, drug use, sexual promiscuity, and violent crime see sharp increases during the teenage years, and they are trickling down to affect ever younger children.

Our culture has no answer to such despair. But the church does. It is time for Christian adults to step forward and offer our love and the hope of the Gospel.

What can we promise children and young people that will counter their dangerous despair and self-destruction? We need to bombard them with scriptural hope. My sister, Hope Toole, has known from childhood that her name has a special meaning. "Hope" is found in the promised return of Jesus Christ to redeem His church (Titus 2:13). But the hope found in Christ also grants fulfillment and joy to our lives today, not just at some future day. When Satan traps adults or children in a gloomy view of the world, he has succeeded in turning their eyes away from God. Yet God has redeemed our present and granted us unimaginable future glory.

Why can you and your students have hope, even in troubled times?

God is good. America, the richest nation in the world, is a country of pessimists. Christians often lead the pack in negative thinking, because we have a clearer sense of the troubles and sins of the world around us. We forget, in our everyday awareness of man's fallenness, how grand is our salvation and how glorious our God. Gratitude is a skill we all need to recover. Worship that is based on the character of God renews hope.

God is in control. Young children believe this, and they trust. Older boys and girls and teens need to continue to worship a God who is not surprised by circumstances. Teachers must consciously point students toward that bigger God of the Bible, the God who knows in advance everything that will happen—and can handle it.

Life has purpose. Randomness and hopelessness go together. If a person believes human beings are here by chance, that human life has a negative effect on the Earth, and that our genetic programming means we cannot control our behavior or our future, he or she cannot have much hope. Boys and girls are often given enormous amounts of data concerning impending environmental disasters and other catastrophes. But the Bible says man is a deliberate creation of God (made in His image), that Christ died to restore and forgive fallen man, and that we are here on purpose to worship and serve God. In fact, individual believers have been given different spiritual gifts so that each person—young or old—matters in the church.

I have a future. People who believe they have a future don't throw their present away. I remember from childhood lying in bed actually longing and crying for Christ's return because I wanted to see Him so badly. Those who know that their future is guaranteed are also freed to face today's harsh realities, even when that means bearing up under persecution. And hope for the future reminds us of God's goodness today.

I am loved, and I am protected. Children often feel they are outsiders, even when they're not. It's a rare junior high kid who actually *feels* popular. Children and young people need more than the changeable acceptance of their peers. They also need the consistent, mature love of adults and the knowledge of God's abiding love. The world of children can be a nasty, brutal one of fighting for one's place and making hard choices to retain friends. Your love, the safety you offer, and your reassurance of God's love can lend strength to the child who needs it.

Parents and teachers need to offer children the hope that comes only through the Gospel. I like Ron Hutchcraft's metaphor that working with young people is not helping on a playground but working in a battlefield. Our task is to equip children who are in love with their King to follow Him. To do our job well, we must often make a deliberate choice to do things in a way our culture (and even much Christian curriculum) would say will never work. We cannot rely on culturally approved methods to train countercultural children who will resist the things that fascinate and destroy their peers and who will choose, instead, the hope found in Christ.

How does a teacher train godly, countercultural children who are alive with the hope of Christ? By making deliberate choices. Those choices aren't always easy, but they're essential to good teaching.

- Get to know your children.
- Make your class a safe place for children.
- Teach your children to study—and love—Scripture.
- Take lesson preparation seriously.
- Use every part of your lesson time, including the music, thoughtfully, not just as filler or entertainment.
- Know your students' world; cry over it or laugh with them in it.
- Pray with them and for them. Teach them to pray.
- Connect them with God directly.
- Don't bring God down to their level.
- Lead them. Give them hope. Give them a mission. Give them a future.

May the God of peace, who through the blood of the eternal covenant brought back from the dead our Lord Jesus, that great Shepherd of the sheep, equip you with everything good for doing his will, and may he work in us what is pleasing to him, through Jesus Christ, to whom be glory for ever and ever. Amen. (Hebrews 13:20–21 NIV)

APPENDIX A:
Sample Bible Studies for Children

Ten Commandments

This can work as review after studying the Ten Commandments. Break boys and girls into separate groups, and give each group the following assignment: "Your cousin doesn't know what the Ten Commandments mean or why they are important. Your cousin is seven years old. How would you explain the first five [or the last five] commandments to her [for the boys, him]?"

I said "cousin" because I used this in an African-American church, where children were quite likely to know their cousins and thus even an only child or the youngest in a family could relate to the assignment. You could use "friend." I made the cousin slightly younger than the children themselves so that my students would be trying to simplify the commands. After fifteen or twenty minutes, I called both groups together and had one child explain each command.

Paul's Journeys

I found seven passages that talked about Paul's journeys in language that could be understood by younger children. (The class was second and third graders.) The passages were: Acts 11:28–30; Acts 13:2–5; Acts 16:20–31; Acts 17:1–5, with 16:25; Acts 18:1–4; Acts 21:1–6; and Acts 23:23–24, with verses 18–21.

I made an index card for each passage and wrote the following questions on each:

1. Where did Paul go?
2. Who went with him? (Note that the "with" passages are sometimes necessary for this question. When they were, I wrote "See Acts _____" in parentheses. The Acts 21:1–6 passage says only "we," so I explained to the student who got that card that Luke wrote Acts.)
3. What did they do? (For the Acts 23:23–24 passage, instead of this question I wrote, "Why did those people go with him? To find out, read Acts 23:18–21.")

I gave each child a separate index card, but pairs of children would have worked well with this exercise. I walked around the room with a map to let each child see where Paul traveled in his Scripture passage. If I had been working with older children I could have had them report back to the larger group.

Attributes of God

I used this with junior-age girls and tried to match up girls who weren't very confident in their use of the Bible with girls who were. I gave each pair a different attribute and the following instructions: "What does ____ [passage] say about ____ [the attribute—for example, God's love]? What other passages from the Bible can you find that talk about ____ [God's love]?" I encouraged the girls to find verses that told about the attribute and verses that showed God using it—for instance, a time when Jesus showed love. I wandered around the room helping girls think of stories and passages, then they reported back to the group. Some attributes and passages you might use include the following:

Truth, faithfulness (He keeps His promises): Numbers 23:19; Hebrews 10:23; 2 Timothy 2:13
Love: Psalm 145:15–16; Luke 7; Acts 14:17; Romans 5:8
Holiness (above everything He has made; perfect): Psalm 99; Isaiah 55:9; Habakkuk 1:13a; Revelation 4:8
Sovereignty (power, freedom to do anything; being in charge): Deuteronomy 10:14, 17; Job 26:6–14; Psalm 115:3; Isaiah 66:1; Mark 4:35–41; Luke 1:37
Justice (doing the right thing): Genesis 18:25; Deuteronomy 32:4
Grace (giving good things we don't deserve): Ephesians 2:8–9; Titus 3:4–7

Some other attributes include unchanging, all-knowing (omniscient), present everywhere (omnipresent), existing forever (eternal). Exodus 34:6–7 and Jeremiah 10:10 are good verses to include, because both passages list several attributes.

If you want to explore actions of God as shown in His roles, try these: Creator, Savior, Protector, Teacher, Judge.

By the way, I developed this because two or three times I've had children of this age plead with me for the chance to lead their own devotional time. (I have also asked children of that age to come prepared to tell and explain their favorite Bible verse.)

The Lord's Supper

I had two purposes in doing this as a sword drill with my second- and third-grade class: teaching basic Bible skills and looking at several passages that talk about Communion. Because many of my students weren't very familiar with the Bible yet, I wrote the names of the first eight books of the New Testament on the chalkboard and went over them with the children. Then I allowed them to put a marker in Matthew.

I told the child who found the verse first to wait until everyone got to it before reading it aloud. I used the following verses: Luke 22:8; Matthew 26:26–28; Luke 22:19; Mark 14:23; Matthew 26:29; 1 Corinthians 10:16; 1 Corinthians 11:25. (It's worth noting that the following week, when I asked in a review game, "What are three books of the Bible that talk about Communion?" the boys were able to tell me Matthew, Mark, and 1 Corinthians.)

Other Passages

Other passages that lend themselves well to classroom-guided studies include

1. **Psalm 119** (What words does this long chapter use to describe the Bible?)
2. **Isaiah 53 or Psalm 22** (How does this text—written hundreds of years before Jesus was born—describe His crucifixion?)
3. **Hebrews 11** (Have children compare the summaries of these men and women of faith with the Old Testament accounts.)
4. **1 Corinthians 13** (What does it mean to love?)

What are some of the things children in the church need to know?

1. **Truths:** who God is and what He is like (attributes, action, the Trinity); the Gospel (sin, who Christ is, what He did); the church (reason, functions, history, etc.—most churches assume members know this, but we rarely actually teach from Acts or the Epistles, especially in the lower grades); an overview of Scripture
2. **Facts:** books of the Bible (at least the basics), selected verses, Ten Commandments, and so on.
3. **Skills:** Bible memory, Bible familiarity (reading, studying, putting the pieces together), prayer, talking about God (witnessing and fellowship), obeying God

APPENDIX B:
Starting a Teacher Training Program at Your Church (and using this book in such a program)

I wrote *Follow Me As I Follow Christ* because I realized that the vast majority of churches either lack teacher training or need a more focused teacher training program. I hope this book will help fill the gap, both by helping individual teachers and by helping churches establish programs of training. If you are a volunteer teacher rather than a staff member at your church, you may find these notes helpful in drafting a memo to your church leaders that explains the need for training. If you are in a position to begin teacher training, this appendix should provide some ideas for using this book in such a program.

What steps are needed to launch teacher training?

Whether you are a layperson or you are on pastoral staff, several steps are necessary for beginning a training program.

1. Establish a need. Find out through questionnaires or interviews where your teachers need help.
2. Solicit resources. Budget for the need; recruit speakers; collect materials.
3. Decide procedures. You need to decide time and date, frequency, length of meetings, etc.
4. Advertise. Let your teachers know about the teaching that will soon be offered.
5. Prepare. Finalize everything.
6. Execute. Teach the program.
7. Evaluate. Ask for feedback. Find out how the teaching has helped your teachers.

Why do volunteer teachers need training?

1. We cannot assume that experienced teachers are good teachers. I have seen dreadful veteran teachers. And even good teachers can improve.
2. The teacher training most churches offer, if they have any at all, is irregular, infrequent, and focused on peripheral subjects. A training program needs to begin with the basics.
3. Some church members who currently do not teach probably would do so if they felt qualified. We need to equip them.
4. We need to show teachers and parents that our children are important to us. Training teachers demonstrates that.
5. We need to guard against our students learning false doctrine—whether false teaching is actually taught in the classroom or whether they misunderstand their teachers as a result of poor communication.
6. We need to be sure our teachers have an adequate philosophy of teaching and adequate knowledge of what to teach and how to teach.
7. We need to be deliberate about our philosophy of education. Our first resource is the Bible, not the teacher's guide. Our goal is Christian education, not entertainment. Our first criterion for methodology is truth, not whether it "works" or whether it is fun.
8. Most church programs need more volunteers, and in many cases they particularly need more men. But before placing more leaders in any program, we need to train them.

How can we find time to train busy teachers?

The following list suggests a possible approach for eventually involving all your teachers in some form of training:

Step one: If possible, require all teachers to come early for a short, regular training session. This could be as brief as fifteen minutes of focused attention on one subject.

Step two: Extend church membership classes by about four weeks for those who have some interest in teaching. This trains them *before* they have made other commitments to the Sunday school hour, and it encourages those with dedication and some interest, but little or no experience, to consider teaching. Such a course would cover the *basics* of teaching, not extras.

Step three: Evaluate current teachers for effectiveness, knowledge, and skill level. Find out their weaknesses, and customize a training program that emphasizes the basics but that goes beyond them where a need is present.

Step four: Use substitutes or even suspend Sunday school for a month. But somehow free all regular teachers for a four- to six-week training series based on the needs that have been discovered among your teachers. Bring children's church workers and club teachers into the training also.

Step five: Continue to offer the beginning training to new and prospective teachers. In addition, set up a *regular* training program (every three or six months, perhaps) in which subjects beyond the basics could be explored. These training sessions could be optional, and subjects should be announced one or two weeks in advance. If the training is held during Sunday school, substitutes should be readily available. Also, all teachers should be regularly, discreetly evaluated. No teacher should be granted a lifetime "license to teach."

How can this book be used in teacher training?

A suggested format:

If possible, have teachers read a given chapter in advance and consider the questions at the end of the chapter. Open the meeting with prayer. Discuss teachers' observations or their answers to questions. Spend time practicing the skill discussed, or have a speaker teach on the subject. Give assignments, and close in prayer for your teachers and their students.

Basic subjects	Chapters in this book that address this subject
1. How to prepare a lesson (preparing from the Bible itself, then finding additional help in the teacher's guide)—hands-on time is needed here	#32—"Fifteen Minutes to Prepare" #33—"Lesson Planning, Part One: Teaching What the Bible Teaches" #34—"Lesson Planning, Part Two: Two Important Questions" #35—"When Is Application of Scripture Dangerous?" #36—"Application That Fits"
2. How to teach a lesson (hands-on needed)	#38—"Communicating on a Child's Level" #39—"Telling a Bible Story, Part One: Some Guidelines; #40—"Telling a Bible Story, Part Two: A Story's Power" #41—"Effective Use of Visual Aids" #37—"Teaching by Asking Questions" #42—"Teaching Children to Study the Bible" #4—"Teaching What the Bible Teaches"

3. How to communicate the Gospel, give an invitation, and lead a child to Christ	#46—"Explaining the Gospel, Part One: "The Importance of the Right Words" #47—"Explaining the Gospel, Part Two: The Process" #48—"Leading a Child to Christ"
4. How to discipline effectively, including at least minimal instruction in child development	#14—"Is It Sin or Immaturity?" #18—"Learning Humility and Patience" #19—"Respecting Children" #20—"Teaching Children Respect" #21—"Being the Adult in the Classroom" #23—"Moving into Your Students' World" #26—"Dealing with Disinterested Kids" #43—"Working with Kids Who Blow the Curve" #13—"Knowing the Characteristics of Age Groups" #51—"Working with Your Students' Parents"
A few ideas for teaching that goes beyond the basics	**Chapters in this book that address this subject** *(Also see Appendix C: For Further Reading.)*
1. Teaching with use of memory verses, songs, crafts, review games, small groups, one-on-one interaction time, or other parts of the program	#44—"Teaching Children to Pray" #45—"Teaching Memorization" #27—"Interacting with the Child Who Really Needs You"
2. Developing creativity and developing a teaching style	#21—"Being the Adult in the Classroom" #23—"Moving into Your Students' World" #26—"Dealing with Disinterested Kids" #38—"Communicating on a Child's Level"
3. Discipleship	#50—"Follow Me As I Follow Christ" #52—"Connecting Children to the Church" #2—"Who Is This God We Teach? Part One: God's Holiness"

	#3——"Who Is This God We Teach? Part Two: God's Love" #23——"Moving into Your Students' World" #25——"Encouraging the Irregular Attendee" #27——"Interacting with the Child Who Really Needs You" #22——"Wanted: Christian Men in the Classroom"
4. Understanding children; understanding *your church's* children	#6——"What Scripture Says About Children" #8——"Children Without Childhood" #9——"Not a Sentimental Affair" #10——"Developing a Broken Heart" #11——"The Wonder of Childhood" and #12——"The Faith of a Child" #14——"Is It Sin or Immaturity?" #24——"Understanding Across Cultural Lines" #38——"Communicating on a Child's Level"
5. Developing your own Bible-study skills	#35——"When Is Application of Scripture Dangerous?" #36——"Application That Fits" #2——"Who Is This God We Teach? Part One: God's Holiness" #3——"Who Is This God We Teach? Part Two: God's Love" #4——"Teaching What the Bible Teaches" #33——"Lesson Planning, Part One: Teaching What the Bible Teaches" #34——"Lesson Planning, Part Two: Two Important Questions"
6. More specialized topics (e.g., working with kids with unique problems, sociology, specific ages, etc.)	#24——"Understanding Across Cultural Lines" #25——"Encouraging the Irregular Attendee" #26——"Dealing with Disinterested Kids"

Basic subjects	Ideas for teaching this subject/ Priority for teaching this subject	In-class activities/ Homework assignments	Other resources/ Good speaker(s) for this subject
1. how to prepare a lesson			
2. how to teach a lesson			
3. how to communicate the Gospel, give an invitation, and lead a child to Christ			
4. how to discipline effectively, including at least minimal instruction in child development			
Beyond the basics			
1. teaching with other parts of the program			
2. developing creativity and developing a teaching style			
3. discipleship			
4. understanding children; understanding your church's children			
5. developing your own Bible-study skills			
More specialized topics			
1.			
2.			
3.			
4.			

APPENDIX C:
For Further Reading

Teaching Children in the Church

Gary Bredfeldt and Larry Richards, *Creative Bible Teaching* (Chicago: Moody, 1997). This is an extensive book intended for professionals and students. It is a broad overview of teaching from two experts in the field, not specifically geared to teaching children but useful.

Marva J. Dawn, *Is It a Lost Cause? Having the Heart of God for the Church's Children* (Grand Rapids: Eerdmans, 1997).The author's passion for seeing children as an important part of the church comes through strongly in this book.

Mark DeVries, *Family-Based Youth Ministry* (Downers Grove, Ill.: InterVarsity, 1994). The author explores the significance of considering youth (especially teenagers) as members of families and recognizing that parents hold the primary role in their children's spiritual education. Many practical ideas are presented, but the biblical foundation for an understanding of the church's working with parents is perhaps its most valuable contribution.

Ed Dunlop, *"How Do I Get These Kids to Listen?" Practical Ways to Gain and Hold Attention in the Classroom* (Murfreesboro, Tenn.: Sword of the Lord, 1997). This book is written primarily for those who teach children's church, but it can be readily used by teachers in any church program. It focuses on specific ways a teacher can help or hurt a class's ability to listen. Topics range from use of visual aids to the way the room is set up and a teacher's ability to structure a class hour without large gaps of time in which children can start fidgeting or talking.

Cathy Mickels and Audrey McKeever, *Spiritual Junk Food: The Dumbing Down of Christian Youth* (Mukilteo, Wash.: WinePress, 1999). If you have any say over your church's curriculum, this book will alert you to dangerous things happening under the guise of "Christian" curriculum. An important book, though occasionally nitpicking.

Good Resource Books for

Specific Areas of Teaching

Ethel Barrett, *Storytelling: It's Easy* (Grand Rapids: Zondervan, 1965). This is the classic book on the fundamental art of the Christian teacher of children. Through use of numerous story examples and discussion of everything from preparing the story and understanding the audience to using your voice effectively, *Storytelling* guides the teacher to effective use of this powerful tool.

Eleanor L. Doan, compiler, *Make-It-Yourself Visual Aid Encyclopedia* (Ventura, Calif.: Gospel Light, 1961). This book has instructions and simple drawings to illustrate 350 different types of visual aids the teacher can make. Under "puppets," for example, a few ideas include instructions for making puppets from a stuffed animal, a paper bag, or an ice-cream carton.

Ed Dunlop, *Mouse on a Mission: 54 Bible Review Games to Reinforce Your Lesson* (Murfreesboro, Tenn.: Sword of the Lord, 1999). With the ideas ranging from overhead projector games to chalkboard games to games that can be used on a bus, this is a good resource for teachers who want to incorporate lesson review time in a way children will appreciate.

52 Ways to Teach Bible Reading, 52 Ways to Teach Memory Verses (San Diego: Rainbow Books, 1995, 1996). These reproducible $8^1/_2$-by-11 paperback books are two good ones in a series for primary and junior children. Many of the activities are worthwhile, and they have good variety.

Helen W. Gramelsbach, *71 Creative Bible Story Projects* (Cincinnati: Standard, 1983). This book gives projects (and patterns) for specific stories: for example, Paul in a basket for the story in Acts 9:22–25. Most of the activities can be used either for visual aids or for craft projects.

Bev Gundersen, *Through the Bible in a Year* (Cincinnati: Standard, 1993). Although this book is intended to be used as curriculum, I find it more valuable as a resource providing ideas to use along with lessons I'm teaching. The 52 lessons on significant stories from the Bible give a broad overview of the Bible and a good chance the book will cover a particular lesson.

Howard G. and William D. Hendricks, *Living by the Book* (Chicago: Moody, 1991). This volume will help a teacher who has no idea where to start in studying the Bible.

Barbara Lockwood, *Fun Ideas for Bible Memory* (Cincinnati: Standard, 1989). The ideas for teaching memory verses range from place mats to music to mazes.

Daniel H. Smith, *How to Lead a Child to Christ* (Chicago: Moody, 1987). This helpful small book looks at the fundamentals of leading a child to Christ. It deals with the basic needs of children and methods for introducing boys and girls to Christ.

Anita Reith Stohs, *Chalkboard Games for the Christian Classroom* (St. Louis: Concordia, 1996). This book is actually broader than the title suggests. It includes a few games, but it also gives various suggestions for creative, simple illustrations teachers can use on the chalkboard to illustrate lessons.

Understanding or Rearing Children

(mostly written for parents)

Johann Christoph Blumhardt and Christoph Friedrich Blumhardt, *Thoughts About Children* (Rifton, N.Y.: Plough, 1980). This is a good little book with a lot of loving wisdom regarding children. The elder Blumhardt believed, for example, that adults spend too much time saying no to children on trivial things. He believes in discipline, but he believes in loving children as Jesus did.

Robert C. Crosby, *Now We're Talking: Questions That Bring You Closer to Your Kids* (Colorado Springs: Focus on the Family, 1996). This book lists hundreds of questions to ask children of various ages to help an adult get to know a child and to start good conversations on everything from school to moral issues or a kid's interests.

Terry W. Glaspey, *Children of a Greater God* (Eugene, Ore.: Harvest House, 1995). This covers various aspects of rearing moral, creative, well-educated children; complete with an annotated bibliography of good children's books.

Gladys Hunt, *Honey for a Child's Heart: The Imaginative Use of Books in Family Life* (Grand Rapids: Zondervan, 1989). The revised edition of this book has an extended annotated bibliography of children's books that alone is worth the price of the book. The author goes into the teaching possibilities of various types of children's books, including fairy tales. She includes a chapter with helpful hints on having family devotions.

William Kilpatrick, *Why Johnny Can't Tell Right from Wrong and What We Can Do About It* (New York: Touchstone, 1992). The author looks at a lot of the forces affecting childhood today, including education. It helped me understand the amorality of many of the children I teach.

Michael and Diane Medved, *Saving Childhood: Protecting Our Children from the National Assault on Innocence* (New York: HarperCollins, 1998). The authors believe strongly in protecting childhood innocence. They discuss numerous examples of how the innocence of children is under assault today from books, movies, school, and other aspects of popular culture, and even from parenting trends. One point that caught my attention was that a child in America has a one-in-one-million chance of being kidnaped by a stranger, yet parents so carefully instill "stranger danger" in their children that boys and girls become unfriendly to adults and far too reliant on their peers, who pose a much greater danger. The final chapter is a tribute to childhood that ends the book on a positive note.

Neil Postman, *The Disappearance of Childhood* (New York: Vintage, 1982, 1994). That Postman is not a Christian created a definite blind spot in the writing of this book. A lot of the good things he credits to literacy could more readily be credited to Christianity. The first half of the book gets long, especially because of this. But the book revolutionized my understanding of childhood and adulthood in America. His insightful list of solutions could have been written by a believer.

Glenda Revell, *Glenda's Story: Led by Grace* (Lincoln, Neb.: Gateway to Joy, 1994). This is a very moving short autobiography, written by a woman who experienced horrendous childhood abuse. Her book focuses on God's care for her, not on her abuse. It's an excellent book for developing a heart for children who really need the love of God manifested through you.

Doris Van Stone and Erwin Lutzer, *Dorie: The Girl Nobody Loved* and *No Place to Cry: The Hurt and Healing of Sexual Abuse* (Chicago: Moody, 1979, 1990). Dorie grew up in foster care: unwanted, unloved, and even abused. Yet God's grace reached her, and now her books minister to other young people who experience rejection and help adults know how to love and help such children.

Walter Wangerin, Jr., *Little Lamb Who Made Thee?* (New York: HarperCollins, 1993). This is filled with beautiful essays and stories on the author's own childhood and that of his children.

An Assortment of Excellent Books for Children

(to help you understand the age group you teach or for resource help)

Preschool Children, Christian

Ella K. Lindvall, *Read-Aloud Bible Stories,* four vols. (Chicago: Moody, 1982–95) and *Parables Jesus Told* (Chicago: Moody, 2000). Each book has several full-color stories from the Bible using very simple language. They are favorites of many children. My roommate and I were astonished how long some girls coming by our house—much too old for these books—continued to choose them over any of the other books I had.

Julia Miner, illustrator, *The Shepherd's Song* (New York: Dial, 1993). The illustrator chose a South American shepherd family, their sheepdog, and their sheep (including one ever-straying lamb) for a beautiful, large-format book whose words are limited to Psalm 23 in the King James version.

L. J. Sattgost, *When the World Was New* (Sisters, Oreg.: Questar, 1996). This book tells the story of creation in rhyme—sometimes a bit too sing-songy, but decently done and with breathtaking watercolors. Two or three pages of birds just explode with color.

Grade-School Children, Christian

Paul Hutchens, Sugar Creek Gang series (Moody Press, recently updated). These books have been in print for up to fifty years, and the thirty-six books in the series are all still popular. They are good adventure stories, and the narrator (a boy about ten) and six friends are always learning new things about what it means to be a Christian.

Jon Knapp II, *A Pillar of Pepper* (Elgin, Ill.: Chariot Books, 1982). This has various stories from the Bible told as poetry. (Summary of the title poem: Lot's wife became a pillar of salt. On the other hand, when Miriam disobeyed God she became a leper, not a pillar of pepper.) Some are very good, some mediocre, but the book is worth getting hold of because it brings a fresh approach to stories that easily become stale.

C. S. Lewis, Narnia series (New York: HarperCollins, 1950–56) Seven books. Junior age—all ages, really. Some of the best books for children ever written, with the double delight that Lewis was deliberately writing to make children see Christianity as a thing of beauty.

————, *Letters to Children* (New York: Touchstone, 1985). These letters to children who had written to Lewis discuss everything from prayer to writing. They show an excellent example of an adult who treated children as serious and fully human, not as cute little ones whose questions amuse grown-ups. "By the way, always remember that old people can be quite as shy with young people as young people can be with old. That explains what must seem to you the idiotic way in which so many grown-ups talk to you" (p. 25).

Carolyn Nystrom, Follow the Leader series (Chicago: Moody, 1998). Characters are Esther, Joseph, Elijah, and Jonah. I think these are better than almost anything else available. They are true to Scripture, yet well told. They have stunning artwork. The ten-year-olds I work with like these books, which are written for a higher level than preschool and first grade, though they are picture books. The characters are clearly Jewish, and the pictures have beautiful touches (Esther has a Persian cat in almost every picture once she gets to the palace).

Helen L. Taylor, *Little Pilgrim's Progress* (Chicago: Moody, n.d.). A child-friendly retelling of the old classic that fascinates early elementary-school children.

Grade School, not explicitly Christian

Aesop's fables. Various versions available, teaching moral lessons with short memorable parables.

Carlo Collodi, *Pinocchio* (unabridged version). Adapted versions have Pinocchio as lovingly irresponsible. But in the original, Pinocchio learns lessons about sloth, greed, selfishness, etc., in a well-told story.

Johanna Spyri, *Heidi* (various translations). I struggled through this in first grade—it took me a month—then reread it at least once a year for the rest of my childhood. It's a very good story of a child in the Swiss Alps who lives with her crusty old grandpa and makes friends with the local goatherd, in the process reminding her grandfather of his need for God and for other people.

Laura Ingalls Wilder, Little House series (New York: HarperCollins, 1932–43). Junior girls. Not only is this series of nine books insightful and interesting, but they are also very moral. For instance, Laura is delighted at Christmas to find her stocking contains an orange, a tin cup, a stick of candy, and a penny. A child who is discontent with her own $200 worth of Christmas gifts should really see a contrast.

Junior High, Christian

John Bunyan, *Pilgrim's Progress* (various publishers). Even better, find a good revision and introduce it as a book read aloud to children. Those who grow up with it love it, but I still find it hard to get through (my problem, not the book's).

Hannah Hurnard, *Hinds' Feet on High Places* (Wheaton, Ill.: Tyndale, 1986)—It's the rare girl or woman who doesn't love this book with its imagery of the Christian life.

George MacDonald's fairy tale novels for children: *At the Back of the North Wind, The Princess and the Goblin, The Princess and Curdie,* and *The Lost Princess* (incidentally, a very good book for adults, with great wisdom in child-rearing). C. S. Lewis credits MacDonald with awakening his "moral imagination," a process that eventually led to Lewis's conversion.

J. R. R. Tolkien, *The Hobbit* and *The Lord of the Rings* (various publishers). Although these books are not explicitly "Christian," the author's strong Christian understanding resulted in powerful depictions of good versus evil, the lure and the danger of sin, the joy of common things, and the privilege of relationships.

A Few Good Devotionals for Children

Jesse Lyman Hurlbut, *Hurlburt's Story of the Bible* (Grand Rapids: Zondervan, 1967). Also available in a 1974 revised edition.

W. Phillip Keller, *A Child's Look at the 23rd Psalm* (New York: Doubleday, 1981).

Ella K. Lindvall, *Read-Aloud Bible Stories* 1-4 (Chicago: Moody, 1982-1995) and *Parables Jesus Told* (Chicago: Moody, 2000).

Carolyn Nystrom, Children's Bible Basics series (Moody Press, various years)—a series answering such questions as, "Why do I do things wrong? and, "Who is Jesus?"

Kenneth N. Taylor, *The Bible in Pictures for Little Eyes* (Chicago: Moody, 1956, 1984).

_____, *Devotions for the Children's Hour* (Chicago: Moody, 1987).

_____, *Small Talks About God* (Chicago: Moody, 1958, 1985).

Family Night Tool Chest (three or more books, published by Victor).

Keys for Kids (two-month devotionals published by Children's Bible Hour, Box 1, Grand Rapids, MI 49501; one copy free by request).

Note: You should also read a few of the current books your students are reading to get an idea of what they are being exposed to. By third grade or so, "trendy" books tend to be published in series. Examples: American Girls, Babysitters Club, Goosebumps. In February 2000, I looked up the category "children's horror" on Amazon.com and was told of 2,494 matches!